IT SUPPORT OF THE JUDICIARY

Australia, Singapore, Venezuela,
Norway, The Netherlands and Italy

Series Editors

Aernout H.J. Schmidt, *Editor-in-Chief*
Center for eLaw@Leiden, Leiden University

Berry J. Bonenkamp, *Managing Editor*
NWO/IT*e*R, The Hague

Philip E. van Tongeren, *Publishing Editor*
T·M·C·ASSER PRESS, The Hague

For other titles in the Series see p. 147

INFORMATION TECHNOLOGY & LAW SERIES ④

IT SUPPORT OF THE JUDICIARY

Australia, Singapore, Venezuela, Norway, The Netherlands and Italy

edited by

Anja Oskamp, Arno R. Lodder and Martin Apistola

Computer/Law Institute
Vrije Universiteit Amsterdam

contributions by

Martin Apistola
Marco Fabri
Morten S. Hagedal
Ronald van den Hoogen
Ricardo Jiménez
Arno R. Lodder
Anja Oskamp
Thian Yee Sze
Anne Wallace

T·M·C·ASSER PRESS
The Hague

The *Information Technology & Law Series* is published
for ITeR by T·M·C·Asser press
P.O. Box 16163, 2500 BD The Hague, The Netherlands
<www.asserpress.nl>

T·M·C·Asser press English language books are distributed exclusively by:

Cambridge University Press, The Edinburgh Building, Shaftesbury Road,
Cambridge CB2 2RU, UK,
or
for customers in the USA, Canada and Mexico:
Cambridge University Press, 40 West 20th Street, New York, NY 10011-4211, USA

<www.cambridge.org>

The *Information Technology & Law Series* is an initiative of ITeR, the National Programme for
Information Technology and Law, which is a research programme set up by the Dutch
government and the Netherlands Organisation for Scientific Research (NWO) in The Hague.
Since 1995 ITeR has published all of its research results in its own book series. In 2002 ITeR
launched the present internationally orientated and English language *Information Technology
& Law Series*. This series deals with the implications of information technology for legal
systems and institutions. It is not restricted to publishing ITeR's research results. Hence,
authors are invited and encouraged to submit their manuscripts for inclusion. Manuscripts and
related correspondence can be sent to the Series' Editorial Office, which will also gladly
provide more information concerning editorial standards and procedures.

Editorial Office
NWO / ITeR
P.O. Box 93461
2509 AL The Hague, The Netherlands
Tel. +31(0)70-3440950; Fax +31(0)70-3832841
E-mail: <iter@nwo.nl>
Web site: <www.nwo.nl/iter>

Single copies or Standing Order
The books in the *Information Technology & Law Series* can either be purchased as single
copies at the regular retail price or through a standing order at a discount. For ordering
information see the information on top of this page or visit the publisher's web site at
<www.asserpress.nl/cata/itlaw4/fra.htm>.

ISBN 90-6704-168-8
ISSN 1570-2782

Cover and lay-out: Oasis Productions, Nieuwerkerk a/d IJssel, The Netherlands

TABLE OF CONTENTS

ABBREVIATIONS

AIJA	Australian Institute of Judicial Administration
AIPA	Authority for Information Technology in the Public Administration
ASIC	Australian Securities & Investments Commission
BISTRO	Bureau Internet Systemen en Toepassingen Rechterlijke Organisatie
CCJ	Council of Chief Justices
CMS	Case Management System
COMPAS	Communicatie Openbaar Ministerie Parket Administratie Systeem
DIS	Document Information System
DPP	Director of Public Prosecutions
EFS	Electronic Filing System
ELRO	Elektronisch Loket Rechterlijke Organisatie
ICT	Information and Communication Technology
ICTRO	ICT-bedrijf Rechterlijke Organisatie / ICT for the Judicial Organisation
IP	Internet Protocol
IT	Information Technology
JIRS	Judicial Information Research System
KM	Knowledge Management
LAN	Local Area Network
PVRO	Programma Versterking Rechterlijke Organisatie

Re.Ge.	Registri Generali
RES	Registri esecuzioni / Execution registry of action
RUG	Rete Unica Giustizia / Justice Unified Network
RUPA	Rete Unica per la pubblica amministrazione
SIDDA	Sistema Informativo Direzione Distrettuale Antimafia / Information System for Anti-mafia District Bureau
SIS	Sentencing Information System
SIDNA	Sistema Informativo Direzione Nationale Antimafia / Information System for Anti-mafia National Bureau
SITUS	Sistema Informativo Tribunali e Uffici di Sorveglianza / Information Systems for Tribunals and Surveillance Offices
SMS	Short messaging services
SQL	Standard query language
TSJ	Tribunal Supremo de Justicia / Supreme Tribunal of Justice
VCAT	Victorian Civil and Administrative Tribunal
WAP	Wireless Application Protocol
XML	eXtensible Markup Language

Chapter 1
INTRODUCTION

Anja Oskamp, Arno R. Lodder and Martin Apistola

1.1 IT SUPPORT OF THE JUDICIARY

Information Technology (IT) has found its way into legal practice and as a part thereof to the Judiciary. In 2001 the ITeR report edited by Lodder, Oskamp and Schmidt provided an overview of the *IT Support of the Judiciary in Europe*.[1] Also in 2001 there appeared a study edited by Fabri and Contini that reported on IT support in the Judiciary in Europe as well.[2] These two reports are mostly complementary, together offering a broad perspective of the use of IT support in the Judiciary of European countries.

The 2001 ITeR report included overviews of the IT support of the Judiciary in Norway, the United Kingdom, the Netherlands, Belgium, France, and Italy. We asked for and received funding to extend our research to other, remaining European countries. However, when commencing that research we decided to take another road,[3] viz., IT support of the Judiciary *outside* Europe, for the following reasons.

First, after applying for and receiving the funding in the summer of 2001 the report by Fabri and Contini was published in the late autumn of 2001. We then thought that reports on other European countries would not add that much to both the report by Fabri and Contini and the previous ITeR report: we did not want to deliver more of the same.

---

[1] A.R. Lodder, A. Oskamp and A.H.J. Schmidt, *IT Support of the Judiciary in Europe*, ITeR No. 43, The Hague, Sdu 2001.

[2] Marco Fabri and Francesco Contini (Eds.), *Justice and Technology in Europe: How ICT is Changing the Judicial Business*, The Hague, Kluwer Law International, 2001.

[3] We took this decision after consulting ITeR, the National Programme for Information Technology and Law.

Second, to our knowledge, there is not that much information available on IT support of the Judiciary in other continents: we wanted to take a first, modest step.

Finally, we expected that, like in Europe, in other continents developments were taking place that would be interesting to report.

Since we already covered Europe, four possible continents were left. Africa was not selected, mainly because we did not have any contacts in African countries. Nonetheless a future overview would be really interesting, because at this moment probably all phases of IT support of the Judiciary can be found in Africa: from none or just starting to really advanced IT support.

This report provides an impression of the three other continents, or, better still, of a country in each of these continents: Australia (Australasia), Singapore (Asia), and Venezuela (South America). We realize that this selection is rather thin. Not as far as Australia is concerned. We presume that other countries in that continent (primarily New Zealand) would not significantly alter the impression of the Australasian continent. The reason we have not included other Asian or American countries is that it appeared not as easy to get people involved as it is Europe, where in most countries one tends to know those people working on this topic. In addition we encountered a language problem, which also turned out to be an important factor in the reluctance of people to participate in this project. Illustrative in this respect is that one of our former project members, who sadly left this project, said that he would arrange representatives from various South America countries. In the end only Jiménez from Venezuala participated. His report is not very detailed, mainly because of the language problem, both in writing and orally. Additional material was only available in Spanish.

Despite all this, we believe that the overviews of the three countries in this book are valuable for those who are interested in legal IT support in general, and IT support of the Judiciary in particular. In Australia the vastness of the country[4] has been one reason to invest in, for instance, IT

---

[4] Although Norway is of course by far not as large as Australia, similar reasons for the use of IT in the judiciary played a role, Morten S. Hagedal, 'Norway: practical perspective', in Lodder, Oskamp and Schmidt 2001, see n. 1.

support as well as, for example, distance hearing by video conferencing. Singapore is interesting since the IT support was used as the means to transform an old-fashioned, poor working Judiciary into a smooth functioning organisation.[5] Venezuela is interesting since a World Bank programme provided financial support to develop courtroom technology as well as other IT support which on several points is more advanced than in, for instance, the Netherlands.

One last remark about our selection of countries concerns North America. An impression of North America would be interesting because a great deal has been achieved there. However, the diversity of these accomplishments is difficult to summarize in a single report. Even an overview of what is happening would be too extensive to fit within the scope of this limited research project. Besides, information about IT support of the Judiciary in the USA is rather easily accessible, for instance via the Internet. The following links, for instance, concerning Courtroom21[6] and the cybercourt of the state of Michigan[7] and the court technology laboratory[8] are worth looking at. Starting in the early nineties, in Courtroom21 all kinds of technology are used, both information technology (e.g., electronic files to retrieve case information, access to the Internet) and more traditional types of technology (e.g., huge TV screens). This use of technology in the courtroom reflects what is commonly referred to as *Courtroom technology*. This report not only deals with courtroom technology, but all the ways in which the Judiciary uses IT.

The Michigan Cybercourt was supposed to be launched in October 2002. A lack of funding prevented this. It is now hoped that it can be launched in 2003.

The Court Technology Laboratory is an initiative of the National Center of State Courts. It organizes, for instance, conferences on courtroom technology on a regular basis.

After a review of the first version of this report it was decided that the report on IT support of the Judiciary outside Europe was to be integrated

---

[5] For an overview in Dutch, including a comparison with the Netherlands, Thian Yee Sze and Arno R. Lodder, 'ICT & de rechterlijke macht van Singapore: waarin een klein land groot kan zijn', *Recht en elektronische media 2002-2*, pp. 30-33.

[6] <www.courtroom21.net>.

[7] <www.michigancybercourt.net>.

[8] <http://ctl.ncsc.dni.us/>.

with part of our report on IT support of the Judiciary in Europe. For that purpose some of the country reports were updated upon our request and then incorporated in this report. The updates were restricted to the following countries: Norway, Italy and the Netherlands. We already stated in the first report that these three countries in our opinion could be qualified as the best equipped and organized with regard to IT for the Judiciary at the end of 2000. The level of IT support in the remaining three countries, France, Ireland and Belgium was significantly lower. A superficial check taught us that in the autumn of 2002 the state of automation had not drastically changed compared to the autumn of 2000. It would be interesting to investigate more thoroughly whether the changes are merely non-existent or are low-profile changes. That, however, was not within the scope of this research.

The remainder of this introduction is structured as follows. First, an outline of this book is provided. Subsequently the state of automation of the Judiciary in various countries of Europe is summarized, based on *IT Support of the Judiciary in Europe*[9] and *Justice and Technology in Europe: How ICT is Changing the Judicial Business*.[10] Then we will provide an overview of and draw some conclusions from the reports contained in the present book. In the final section we will make some general observations in which the various developments inside and outside Europe are discussed in combination. We do not attempt to find common denominators of the use of IT support of the Judiciary in the various countries. It will become clear that the way in which IT has been used to support the Judiciary as well as how it is used in the courtroom is different. The reasons for this may be found in the cultural settings, the differences between the legal systems, and policy choices, to mention but a few. It has become clear, however, that by far not all potential solutions for IT support have been pursued. There are many possibilities left and consequently many choices still have to be made. This report, together with *IT Support of the Judiciary in Europe*, aims to contribute to the discussion on the use of legal IT support, in particular in the Judiciary, and to provide an overview of the various possibilities.

---

[9] Lodder, Oskamp and Schmidt 2001, see n. 1.
[10] Fabri and Contini, see n. 2.

1.2 OUTLINE OF THIS BOOK

Our research was basically organized in the same way as *IT Support of the Judiciary in Europe*. We sent out a questionnaire (see Appendix 1) to delegates from the three selected countries. We asked them to use the questionnaire as a guideline in order to compile reports on selected issues involving IT support within the Judiciary, e.g., regarding courtroom technology and knowledge management. At a workshop held in Leiden (the Netherlands) on 15 June 2001 the reports contained in this book were presented. Not included is the presentation that was delivered by Dory Reiling concerning the IT support of the Judiciary, because this topic had already been covered in *IT Support of the Judiciary in Europe*. Besides this introductory chapter, this book consists of the following chapters:

- a report on Australia by Anne Wallace (chapter 2);
- a report on Singapore by Thian Yee Sze (chapter 3);
- a report on Venezuela by Ricardo Jiménez (chapter 4).

Concerning the last report we have to reiterate that the language problem finally influenced the length and the degree of the details in this report. A great deal of additional material was provided, but unfortunately all in Spanish.

In order to facilitate the comparison, we also decided to include in this book updated versions (March 2003) of the most characteristic reports from *IT Support of the Judiciary in Europe*. These reports can be found in chapter 5 (Norway), chapter 6 (the Netherlands) and chapter 7 (Italy).

1.3 IT SUPPORT OF THE JUDICIARY IN EUROPE

In *IT Support of the Judiciary in Europe* the state of IT support in six different countries was presented, from south to north: Italy, France, the United Kingdom, Belgium, the Netherlands and Norway. Our main conclusion was that the general level of IT use in the courts in the described European countries was fairly adequate. For instance, the Judiciary in all six countries basically use the Internet, as well as exchanging information electronically between the courts. However, the actual level of automation varies significantly. The reasons for this diversity are, as mentioned above, cultural settings, differences in the legal systems, policy choices like government interference, and combinations thereof. There is also a difference between theory and practice, as is often the case with IT use. The fact that systems are available does not mean that they are actually used, or that they are used in an optimal manner. Unless people are 'forced' to use the systems, it merely depends on those in question whether they will actually use the systems and use them in the way intended. Moreover, compelling their use does not help that much either. The actual user should be convinced that IT really provides support and that the use of IT does not mean that the work he/she is doing will be completely taken over by computers and as a consequence the Judiciary would find him/her surplus to requirements.

The three countries that are not updated in this present report can be characterized as follows.

In France the present state of automation in the courts is rather basic. In 1998 a programme was commenced which promotes IT as a tool in order to instigate major changes and which should privide a strong impulse for the use of IT and, indeed, Internet in the courts.

The legal system in the UK differs a great deal from the legal systems in other European countries. In the UK the reforms, named after Lord Woolf, under whose direction the research was carried out and reported upon, were supposed to bring the UK system closer to the other European systems, especially with regard to litigation. These reforms also stressed the importance of implementing IT in the courts, especially the civil justice system. Although IT has not yet made the general impact that was hoped for, it has provided an impulse for the amenability of the courts towards the implementation of new techniques.

Despite the fact that all Belgian judges have laptops, the present state of automation in the Belgium courts is still rather low.

In Norway a centralized approach has been taken. The result is that all the courts have been provided with the same solutions, starting with a database system for land registry. Norway takes pride in being among the countries that have the most widespread use of computers in the courts. Interesting is also that this has resulted in very refined models for caseload measurement.

Italy has a rather long history of implementing IT in the courts. Like in Norway, in Italy the government has provided a great incentive for developing IT support for the courts. There have been many pilot schemes on this subject in Italy, but not all of them have resulted in final implementation.

IT support in the courts in the Netherlands is mainly concentrated on the use of the administrative system for supporting public prosecutions, called COMPAS. There have been recent changes which give the impression that serious attempts are being made to bring the IT support in the courts to a more advanced level (the so-called PVRO[11] programme).

Fabri and Contini collected papers based on a seminar which was held four months after the workshop that was reported in *IT Support of the Judiciary in Europe*. Their aim was more ambitious than the ITeR projects. It resulted in an overview of the level of IT support in the following countries: Finland, Austria, Ireland, Norway, Sweden, Belgium, the Netherlands, Denmark, France, Italy, Germany, England and Wales, Spain, Greece and, outside Europe: Latin America. Their book consists of two parts: the first part contains reports that place somewhat more emphasis on the movements towards e-justice (Finland to Denmark). The second part consists of papers which in the opinion of the editors report on countries in which institutional settings having played a major role in the development of IT in the justice systems (France to Greece).

It is interesting is that they note common trends in the European countries, such as the fact that design, development and implementation of IT projects were merely isolated answers to specific problems. In other words, they were not seen as part of the structure and organization in which they had to operate. Moreover, incorporating IT within the judicial system is rather fragmented and is often restricted to a single department. Fabri and Contini give as an example that prison departments seem to be totally detached from the courts' IT projects. This lack of co-ordination between different organizations seems to be a rather common factor in many legal IT projects.[12]

---

[11] Programme to reinforce the judiciary system.

[12] A. Oskamp, *Rechtsinformatica: Vooruitzien in de informatiemaatschappij*, Deventer, Kluwer, 1998, p. 25.

Another interesting finding concerns case management systems. Fabri and Contini report that all countries in the survey have some kind of case management system. In more centralized countries there is a tendency to look at the whole flow of information in criminal case management systems, i.e., not restricted to the courts, but covering the whole spectrum from police reports to possible incarceration. It also notes that each country starts from scratch, not sharing the different applications that are used in other European countries.

Furthermore, Fabri and Contini indicate that throughout Europe there is a clear distinction between the use of IT by administrative staff and by judges and prosecutors. The latter two are not obliged to undergo any training in the use of IT. Consequently IT tools will mainly be used by those who are already 'computer literate'.

1.4   IMPORTANT ISSUES *OUTSIDE* EUROPE

This section uses the structure of the questionnaire contained in the Appendix to present some highlights from the reports contained in chapters 2-4.

1.4.1   History of IT in the Courts both in and outside Europe

When we look at the history of IT support of the Judiciary in the countries described in this report, we see a huge difference in development. In Australia a basic form of IT was already introduced in the Judiciary in the late 1970s. In the 1980s, amongst other things the use of case management systems followed. Singapore started at the beginning of the 1990s with the introduction of IT within the Judiciary. Venezuela began only recently, in the mid-1990s, to explore the possibilities of IT. This is a similar picture to that obtained from Contini[13] when he describes the cycles of IT diffusion. In the 1980s there was some exploration of IT in most European countries, with a rather strong emphasis on case management systems in the late 1980s, and the early 1990s.

---

[13] Francesco Contini, 'Conclusion: Dynamics of ICT Diffusion in European Judicial Systems', in: Fabri and Contini, see n. 2, pp. 317-331.

In the period 1990-2000 the Australian Judiciary began to use a wide range of IT tools. In Singapore the focus during this period was on case management, but also several innovative technological developments were commenced. During the mid-1990s, the first technology court was completed in Singapore. This technology court is comparable with Court-room21. One interesting feature is that the courtroom offers the parties involved in a procedure access to the Internet and as a consequence they also have on-line access to all kinds of information stored in computers at their office. At the beginning of the millennium a technology court was also introduced in Australia. So in the case of technology courts, Singapore was, despite its late start, even ahead of Australia. A last re-mark which we would like to make regarding this decade is that in the final years the emphasis in Australia was transformed from an experi-mental phase to the actual incorporation of IT in the courts. This phase can be compared to Contini's second cycle: improving governance struc-tures. It also complies with the thesis in ITeR No. 43 that for the success-ful introduction of IT tools within the Judiciary there is a need for strong executive power.

It is interesting to compare this with some European countries. In vari-ous countries, like the UK and France, IT was seen as a tool for bringing about change, enhancing the organization and managing the courts. It did not work as well there as it did in Singapore, where the strong executive power was partly responsible for the sudden leap forwards. In France and the UK the effect was overestimated. This is no different from what can be learned from the practice of automation in other professions. It is well known that the implementation of IT is most successful when it is adapted by the persons who will have to use the tools. This implies that they must see the benefits of using the tools that are provided in relation to the situation they are in. Thus: the implementation of IT in the courts will only be successful if there is clear support from those who are going to use it. This implies that they have to be part of the process from the very beginning. The reports tend to support this thesis. On the other hand, it becomes clear from the reports that strong government interference does speed up the process of implementing IT as support tools in the courts. The success of introducing ICT within the courts depends, so it seems to us, on a delicate balance between executive insight and power (by the government) and professional user input and feedback (by judges

and prosecutors). Another instance of the Dutch 'poldermodel' (consultation model)[14] seems to be appropriate.

Nowadays Australia, Singapore and Venezuela are supported by high-
tech courtrooms. For example, use is made of legal (Internet) networks,
electronic document management and dial-in access. We also see the development and use of video conferencing in both Australian and Singapore courtrooms. For the (near) future we can invisage the exploitation in
all three countries of mark-up languages such as eXtensible Markup Language (XML) and Wireless Application Protocol (WAP) and short mes-
saging services (SMS). These countries seem to have entered Contini's
third cycle: towards e-justice. In that respect these three countries are
ahead of most European countries.

1.4.2   Some distinctive features

Systems for case management appear to be the central issue in the development of IT support for the Judiciary worldwide. Once case management has proven its value, it seems that the implementation of other
support tools becomes easier. The reports on Australia, Singapore and
Venezuela provide some distinctive examples, some of which are only
still in their infancy in European countries. Examples are electronic filing
and the use of electronic documents. To support electronic filing, electronic filing systems are being used. In Europe these techniques are currently being investigated, but are not yet in use. In 1999 the observation
was made that in the Netherlands the discussion on using electronic files
in the Judiciary had been taking place for more than a decade, but implementation had still not occurred.[15] Even in 2002 the Judiciary still did not
use electronic files, although in 2003 some pilot projects in Amsterdam
and Rotterdam have been investigating the possibility of using fully electronic files for some criminal court cases. Besides the (lack of) implementation in some European countries, and amongst them the Netherlands, there is not even a legislative provision for electronic filing. An
important feature of these systems is, at least in Australia and Singapore,

---

[14] This model stems from Dutch politics. The central element is consensus.

[15] A.R. Lodder, A. Oskamp and M.J.A. Duker, *Informatietechnologische ondersteuning binnen het strafprocesrecht*, ITeR No. 36, The Hague, Sdu, 2000.

the use of web-based technology. Besides case management and electronic filing and the use of electronic documents, the Internet also plays an important role in the three countries described in this report. Several legal web sites with information on, amongst other things, the courts and cases have been developed.

Pre-trial management plays a role in both the Australian and Venezuelan courts which make use of planning systems in the form of, respectively, calendars, bookings, time standards and schedules. We also see that video conferencing has become an important aspect of IT support in Australia and Singapore. In this respect these countries are also ahead of most European countries, where video conferencing is only just entering the courtroom. The vast distances within the Australian continent will surely be a factor for necessitating video conferencing. And last but not least, in the case of electronic transcription, Australia seems to be the only country using this technology.

1.4.3 Instigating IT projects

To instigate IT projects (for example the development and deployment of case management systems in courtrooms), several questions play an important role. Examples are how do we finance the project, and who will be involved? These are issues that arose in both ITeR No. 43 and Fabri and Contini 2001. As has been stated in the previous section it was concluded that the government plays an important part in initiating projects, but that success strongly depends on acceptance by those who have to work with it. However, to streamline the more general use of systems, their interconnection and compatibility, some guidelines and especially general support is necessary. In the Netherlands we can see that this has been effectuated by, amongst other things, PVRO. Italy also has some dedicated organizations. Norway has always had a centralized approach. In Australia we see that many courts do not have the resources to develop their own systems and the development of systems not tied to commercial software is unlikely. This is also true for the Venezuelan courts where most systems, except the Internet Portal, have been developed by external software companies.

1.4.4   Influence of IT on Legal Practice

We see that the development and deployment of Information Technology (IT) influences the way legal practice functions. In Australia the issues of IT mainly concern fairness, social justice, evidentiary and cultural matters. However, there has been no empirical research on the use of IT in trials, but experience suggests that it depends on the attitude of judges, prosecutors and lawyers. It is important that, despite the availability of IT, parties should have equality of access to the technology. It is not yet clear how far this should go. Other issues are the level of technology knowledge and the compatibility of different systems. In Venezuela, the influence of IT is more on the content of the law. For example, changes to the criminal code, the development of electronic signature law and issues concerning the legal interpretation of e-mail.

The influence of IT on legal practice is partly dependent on the cultural settings within the countries in question. In ITeR No. 43 we already pointed out that the cultural differences between the countries are vast and they influence the impact of IT on legal practice in various respects. In Belgium, for instance, judges often work at home, thus having traditionally poor access to IT support tools like databases. Moreover, it is more difficult to introduce IT tools for people working at very many different (physical) places. The rise of the Internet and the numerous possibilities which the Internet offers may change this. The magistrates will have to embrace a positive attitude towards these tools. When we compare this to the countries in the other continents, we see that in Australia the vastness of the country initially supported the use of IT and special features like video conferencing.

Another interesting aspect is the different opinions that are held in the various countries regarding the separation of judges and the public prosecutors. In some countries, like France, they obtain the same education and can switch from one role to the other rather easily. In other countries like the Netherlands, judges and prosecutors are much more separated. In Singapore the judges and the public prosecutors are separate organs of the State. Nonetheless, the Lord Chancellor is the head of the Judiciary and at the same time a member of the cabinet. The independence of judges makes it difficult to enforce the use of IT applications, because in that case a central authority is lacking. The prosecution is subordinate and so it can, at least theoretically, be compelled to use IT. There are developments, however, to introduce a central authority for judges also. For instance, in Italy such an authority led to several projects and the Dutch Judiciary wishes to introduce a central council for judges. In Singapore the vast investment in IT for changing the Judiciary was initiated by the Lord Chancellor.

The legal system is also influenced by the selection of case law. In the Netherlands the Judiciary has long been dependant on publishers and software companies. Presently the site Rechtspraak.nl,[16] provided by PVRO and under the auspices of ELRO, has given judges their own medium for the publication of case law. In Australia the Judiciary is generally dependent on publishers. In Australia the development of software mostly takes place 'in-house'. In Venezuela files are provided exclusively to certain publishers. The development of case management systems in Venezuela has been through private firms. The development of the portal of the Judiciary is being carried out by the Judiciary itself. In Singapore access to case law now seems to be dominated by LawNet, a strategic national information network within the legal sector that forms part of the information technology infrastructure of Singapore. It is supervised by the LawNet Council, with members like the Chief Justice as Chairman, the Minister of Law, the Attorney-General, the President of the Law Society of Singapore and the Dean of the Faculty of Law at the National University of Singapore.

IT does not always influence legal practice; on the contrary, new IT is not always being used. A way to stimulate the use of IT is to make its use mandatory. Another important issue when using IT in courtrooms is whether all parties are allowed to use the same IT. In Australia we see that the mandatory use of identical IT systems by judges and public prosecutors has not emerged as an issue, while in Venezuela the prosecutors and judges use different IT.

1.4.5 The drawbacks of introducing IT

Introducing IT within the Judiciary is not inexpensive. That means that strong support for IT within the organization is necessary. One of the

---

[16] <http://www.rechtspraak.nl>.

conclusions in *IT Support of the Judiciary in Europe* was that when users are not convinced of the added value of the tools provided they will not use them. It may even be stronger than this. Employees are sometimes afraid of becoming redundant and of losing their jobs when new IT is introduced. In Venezuela, a country with poverty problems, the high costs of IT and the resistance to the introduction of IT prove to be a major drawback in introducing IT. The problem of costs also plays a role in the Australian courts due to limited budgets. In Singapore the outcome of research that pointed to a better cost effectiveness outcome of the use of IT within the Judiciary was an important reason for actually introducing IT. It is not known whether this cost effectiveness still influences budgets.

1.4.6   Information and knowledge management

Systems providing information and knowledge management are used in Australia, Singapore and Venezuela. In Australia these systems are denoted as Judicial Support systems and case management systems. Venezuela and Australia even have special information and knowledge departments. In Australia, however, only large courts and law firms make use of such departments to support knowledge management. Other knowledge management initiatives are legal (electronic) education in both Venezuela and Singapore and the use of legal forums in Venezuela.

In the Netherlands we can see a trend that especially the larger law firms have their own knowledge management departments, often integrated into existing departments that are charged with filing and distributing information.

1.5   Concluding observations

The reports included here demonstrate that IT has been introduced in the Judiciary on a worldwide basis. We also see that IT is being used as a means to instigate change. This has happened very strongly in Singapore, where IT was clearly used to transform an old-fashioned organization where it was difficult or even impossible to obtain access to case information into a modern organization. But also in Venezuela we can see that changes in the Judiciary, here as a result of a change in the political situation, go hand in hand with introducing IT. Also in the European countries we see that IT is sometimes slowly (like in France and Belgium) and sometimes more rapidly (like in Norway) finding its way to the Judiciary. The strong impact of IT on changes in the Judiciary, as was reported in Singapore, has not been seen in European countries.

It also becomes clear that on a worldwide basis emphasis is being placed on case management systems as the backbone for introducing IT in judicial organizations. This is not surprising since the benefits of IT for this purpose can be clearly demonstrated to those concerned. Still we see that especially Singapore and Venezuela report that there was resistance on the part of the legal profession in the initial phase. In the Netherlands we see that case management systems may eventually evolve into digital files, when all information is digitally delivered or inserted.

The use of the internet both as a means to gather and to spread information is also growing rapidly. Courts diffuse their judgments through the internet, thus creating new sources of information. This leads to an abundance of information and it will be one of the challenges of the near future to be able to handle this information. Mark-up languages like XML, possibly custom-made for legal use, and the development and use of legal ontologies will be topics that deserve closer investigation. But also other telecommunication techniques need to be investigated. The use of SMS, as in Venezuela, has turned out to be very effective.

A final observation concerns the problem of costs. IT support for the Judiciary is now in most countries (somewhat) beyond its initial phase. This implies that basic technology is present and that the focus may now shift to more advanced tools. From a technological point of view there are many opportunities and many potential applications. Most of them are costly and especially when we are looking at more innovative applications we see that funding is still a problem. Illustrative is the delay in launching the cybercourt in Michigan. After a House Bill to this effect was passed in December 2001 the launch of the Michigan Electronic Court was foreseen in October 2002. In July 2002 it was reported that it had been postponed until, hopefully, 2003.

We concluded the introduction to ITeR No. 43 by stating that the best way to enhance the use of IT support tools in the Judiciary would be to have an open discussion thereon, not limited to the boundaries of one particular country, but worldwide. That was our main reason for compiling the reports on the state of IT support in the Judiciary in some countries. Previously we set out some topics for further discussion that we considered notable for the further development of IT in the Judiciary in general and in courtrooms in particular. We still consider most of these topics to be important for further discussion. For that reason we conclude this section by again stating some theses that we consider should give rise to further research in an international perspective. For the sake of implementing discussion we formulate them rather strongly.

- The successful introduction of IT tools within the Judiciary is only possible when strong executive power is available (for instance by the government with sanctions for enforcement), together with strong interest and support on the part of the Judiciary itself.

- When the 'users' of the provided tools are not convinced of their added value they will not use them whatever sanction is imposed.

- IT is a successful tool for instigating changes in the organization of the courts.

- IT tools will generate strategic behaviour and consequently may deteriorate the professional ethos of the Judiciary.

- There is a great difference between criminal law procedure and civil law procedure in relation to the introduction of IT tools within the courts. For criminal law it is possible and necessary to impose the introduction of IT tools. For civil law procedures it suffices to convince the users of their usefulness.

There is a need for models and frameworks provided by judges in order to successfully implement IT support tools.

Chapter 2
AUSTRALIA

Anne Wallace

2.1 Organisation/Structure of the Judiciary

2.1.1 The Courts/Judiciary

Australia is a constitutional federation, consisting of five States (New South Wales, Victoria, Tasmania, Queensland, South Australia and Western Australia), two Territories (Northern Territory and Australian Capital Territory) and a Commonwealth. Each State and inhabited Territory has its own independent system of courts consisting of a Supreme Court, an intermediate court – generally known as the District Court – and local courts of summary jurisdiction.

Australian State and Territory courts have original jurisdiction in all matters brought under State or Territory laws and in matters arising under federal laws, where jurisdiction has been conferred on state or territory courts by the Commonwealth Parliament. Most criminal matters, whether arising under Commonwealth, State or Territory law, are dealt with by State or Territory courts. The Federal Parliament is empowered under the Constitution to invest State courts with Federal jurisdiction.[1]

Federal Courts
The High Court of Australia has appellate jurisdiction in respect of, courts exercising federal jurisdiction, and State Supreme Courts, so in

---

[1] Commonwealth Attorney-General's Department, 'Window on the Law – Australia's Legal System – the Court System' at <http://law.gov.au/auslegalsys/auslegalsys.htm #anchor351470>.

A. Oskamp, et al. (Eds), IT Support of the Judiciary
© *2004, ITeR, The Hague, and the authors*

practice it is the final court of appeal in both civil and criminal jurisdictions. It is also Australia's constitutional court.

The Federal Court of Australia has jurisdiction as is invested in it by laws made by the Commonwealth Parliament. This includes, for example, matters in which a writ of mandamus or prohibition or an injunction is sought against an officer of the Commonwealth Government, bankruptcy, corporations law, industrial relations, taxation and trade practices law. It has appellate jurisdiction in relation to the decisions of single judges of the Court, decisions of the respective Supreme Courts of the Australian Territories, except the Northern Territory, and certain decisions of State Supreme Courts when exercising federal jurisdiction.

Also at Federal Level, the Family Court of Australia deals with the dissolution and nullity of marriage, custody and welfare of the children, maintenance and the settlement of property between the parties to a marriage in Australia.

There is also a Federal Magistrates Service which has jurisdiction in less complex matters in the areas of family law and child support, administrative law, bankruptcy law and consumer protection law.

State and Territory Supreme Courts

The Supreme Courts are the highest State and Territory courts. They deal with the most important civil litigation and the most serious criminal cases. They also exercise appellate jurisdiction from the lower State courts. A Full Court of a Supreme Court can hear appeals from a decision of the Supreme Court when constituted by a single Judge. Jury trial also applies in the Supreme Courts.

State and Territory Intermediate Courts

The intermediate courts (District courts) are presided over by a single Judge and decide the great majority of serious criminal offences where a jury is required to decide the facts of a case.[2] They also deal with civil litigation up to certain monetary limits.

---

[2] In some states, an accused may elect trial by judge alone for certain types of offences.

State and Territory Courts of Summary Jurisdiction
The courts of summary jurisdiction are presided over by a Magistrate and deal with most of the ordinary (summary) offences, such as traffic infringements, minor assaults and street offences. Magistrates also conduct committal proceedings in respect of the more serious (indictable) offences to determine whether there is a *prima facie* case to be determined by a judge and jury, either in an intermediate court or a Supreme Court. Juries are not used in courts of summary jurisdiction. These courts also deal with smaller civil jurisdiction claims.

2.1.2   The Prosecution

In Australia, the judicial and prosecution agencies operate separately and independently of each other. The Judiciary has no role in the investigation and prosecution of criminal charges. Its role is to hear the evidence and determine the outcome of charges.

In most States and Territories, much of the prosecution work in courts of summary jurisdiction, particularly in less complex matters, is undertaken by police prosecutors.

In addition, the Commonwealth, all States and Territories have an independent Office or Director of Public Prosecutions, which institutes and conducts criminal cases on behalf of the Crown before the Supreme and District Courts. They generally also deal with defended indictable matters before Courts of Summary jurisdiction and other more complex defended matters.[3]

2.2   INFORMATION TECHNOLOGY: THE MOST PRESSING ISSUES

2.2.1   Trends in IT

The first stage of the use of Information Technology (IT) in courts in

---

[3] See, e.g., NT Office of the Director of Public Prosecutions web site at <http://www.nt.gov.au/dpp/>, Commonwealth Director of Public Prosecutions web site at <http://www.cdpp.gov.au/cdpp/>, Office of the Director of Public Prosecutions ACT web site at <http://www.dpa.act.gov.au/ag/dpp/dpp1.html>, Director of Public Prosecutions, Tas at <http://www.justice.tas.gov.au/cl/index.htm#DPP>.

Australia was the introduction of basic office software and over two decades ago. This was followed, in the 1980s, by the use of case management systems. These were applied, initially, as part of management processes designed to address backlogs in civil jurisdictions, although case management initiatives have subsequently been extended to criminal jurisdictions.

The major impetus to the use of IT in the courtroom in criminal cases, came from two largely unrelated developments in the 1980s. The first was the aftermath of a number of corporate collapses following an economic recession, which resulted in a number of complex white-collar crime investigations and trials. The need to manage the extensive documentation associated with those proceedings saw the development of litigation support and presentation packages designed to be used in electronic courtrooms. The second development was the recognition of a need to provide a means to take evidence from vulnerable witnesses, e.g., children, at a location removed from the physical environment of the courtroom. It resulted in the use of video conferencing technology to provide audio and visual links between courtrooms and other locations.

Over the past fifteen years, technology has developed to a point where it now offers a range of tools which can assist the administration of justice across the spectrum of cases dealt with by our courts. These range from sophisticated systems to relatively simple 'off the shelf' products.

The last two years in Australia have seen rather less emphasis on experimentation in the use of technology in courts, with more of a focus on 'bedding in' technology and making it part of their daily work.[4] There has been a strong emphasis on the use of the Internet and web browser technology. This includes a proliferation of court web sites and plans in many jurisdictions to introduce electronic-filing. Some specific recent developments and future directions are noted below.

2.2.2 Electronic Courtrooms

To facilitate the presentation of evidence created using computerised litigation systems, new technologies had to be incorporated into the court-

---

[4] Jeff Leeuwenburg and Anne Wallace, *Technology for Justice 2000*, AIJA (2001), 3.

room. Australia has successfully developed a number of high technology electronic courtrooms, mainly for use in complex white-collar crime trials, multi-party civil litigation or lengthy commissions of inquiry. Examples include the systems developed for the *Royal Commission into the New South Wales Police Force*, the *Bond* and *Rothwells* trials in Western Australia,[5] the *Estate Mortgage case*,[6] the *Royal Commissions into the Longford Gas Explosion*[7] and the *Metropolitan Ambulance Service in Victoria*[8] and the recent *Glenbrook Inquiry* in New South Wales.

Typically, these systems involve a networked computer operation in the courtroom providing electronic document management and exhibit handling (with sophisticated storage, imaging, searching and retrieval capabilities) real-time electronic transcript and electronic communications facilities.[9] Some of the more recent, have included an Intranet facility to enable dial-in access for all parties for the case, including transcript, e-mail and access to pleadings and documents.[10] The system used for the Inquiry into the Glenbrook Railway disaster also allowed the addition of audio evidence (recordings from signal operators and train drivers) in digital format, accessible through the database.[11]

Initially, most electronic courts were set up on a temporary basis for specific cases and disbanded at the conclusion of the proceedings. By 1998, there was general acceptance of the view that each court in Australia should have at least one permanent electronic courtroom for long and complex trials.[12] Most jurisdictions now have at least one courtroom spe-

---

[5] Australian Law Reform Commission, *Technology – what it means for Federal Dispute Resolution*, Issues Paper No. 23 (1998) [5.42-5.49].

[6] Justice Tim Smith and Ian Chivers, 'The Estate Mortgage Court System', *Technology for Justice Conference Presentations*, Australian Institute of Judicial Administration (CD-ROM) (1998). Victorian Parliamentary Law Reform Committee, *Technology and the Law*, Report (May 1999) [10.11-10.16].

[7] Victorian Parliamentary Law Reform Committee, *above* n. 6, [10.17-10.21].

[8] See Commission web site at <http://www.masrc.org/>.

[9] Jeff Leeuwenburg and Anne Wallace, *Technology for Justice Report*, AIJA (1999), 8.

[10] This was done in both the Estate Mortgage Case and the Metropolitan Ambulance Royal Commission.

[11] Leeuwenburg and Wallace, *above* n. 4, 9.

[12] Sue McGovern, Director of Information Technology, Consultancy Supreme Systems quoted in B. Howarth, 'Digital technology has its day in court', *The Australian*, Tuesday 15 September 1998, 'Computers/The Cutting Edge', 3.

cifically adapted for use as an electronic courtroom. A number have more.[13]

There have been a number of significant improvements in hardware in the last few years. In particular, the development of large format flat screen monitors that are better suited for courtroom use and improvements in the size of personal computers, their reliability, capacity, and price. A basic courtroom display kit, suitable for semi-portable use and quick to set up, can be put together easily, using a laptop, 4-5 screens, CD-ROM burner, a document camera, scanners and basic cabling.[14]

These developments make the extension of this technology possible into a wider range of cases, other than complex or longer trials. More flexible and adaptable systems also mean that parties and the courts are more able to use various parts of the technology most suited to the needs of their particular case, rather than being obliged to adopt a whole system. For example, the use of document imaging and scanners in the courtroom has been found be useful for all types of cases, regardless of complexity – it enables, for example, a witness to give evidence in relation to a location to easily refer to a map displayed on a screen for all participants to see. This ability to 'size the technology to suit the case' also makes it more likely that technology will be more widely used in the future.

In many jurisdictions now, various aspects of the technology have been incorporated into existing courtrooms. In a typical situation, you may have one or two courts with video conferencing facilities, several with data projection facilities and a variety of other more portable technologies that can be made available in any courtroom.[15]

2.2.3 Pre-trial management

The use of technology to manage the pre-trial, or interlocutory process, is not confined to the use of case management systems. Once there is a basic technology infrastructure in place courts can provide on-line access to

---

[13] Leeuwenburg and Wallace, *above* n. 4, 9-10.

[14] Ibid., 10.

[15] See, e.g., 'Technology available in Criminal Courts (Brisbane)' on Queensland Courts web site at <http://www.courts.qld.gov.au/about/technology.htm>.

court calendars, including facilities to allow lawyers to book trial dates and venues. Such a system is currently operating in the Queensland Supreme Court.[16]

The Federal Court of Australia has recently introduced the concept of a virtual courtroom, or 'e-court', using a combination of e-mail and video conferencing, that allows directions and other orders to be made online.[17]

2.2.4 Electronic filing

Electronic filing is an area where much attention is being directed in Australian courts at the moment, particularly in civil jurisdictions. Successful implementation of e-filing is hoped to have a significant impact on efficiency, reduction of errors and maybe even result in some cost savings.

Electronic filing can mean many things – simple or complex, highly automated, or a partial aid to processing. It includes a simple system where e-mails with attached documents are printed out, then treated the same way as mailed-in documents, or a system where a document is transmitted electronically from a law firm to the court and automatically integrated into the court's case management system.[18]

There are some existing electronic filing systems, but these relate to the downloading of bulk electronic data using dial-in connections, for example, the mass transfer of traffic penalty data from police to the local court. The application of Internet technology in e-filing has been the major development in the last few years and it is the direction in which most Australian courts seem to be heading.

The only such operational system as yet is that developed by the Victorian Civil and Administrative Tribunal (VCAT). It allows data to be entered 'on-line' in matters relating to residential tenancy disputes. The VCAT system provides for registered users – such as landlords or tenants' groups – to access VCAT computers directly, over the Internet,

---

[16] See Queensland Supreme Court web site at <http://www.lawnow.com/Supreme CourtService/Policy.htm>.

[17] See Federal Court of Australia web site at <https://www.secure-cf.corams.com/ fed10prd/php/jcms.php3?a=_1&redir=hard>.

[18] Leeuwenburg and Wallace, *above* n. 4, 8.

lodge applications and receive documents and monitor progress of their cases. Users have quickly taken to using the system.[19] Several courts are currently working on specifications for e-filing systems and there are also a number of implementation projects underway.

Innovation and wider use of electronic filing is likely to be affected by the increased use of Legal XML in document definition, exchange, authentication, and conversion. Currently electronic filing mostly works in a single jurisdiction, according to rules and interfaces established by the regulating authority. Legal XML promises us the ability to make it work across jurisdictions and across software platforms.[20]

2.2.5   Transcript – The Court Record

Probably the most readily accepted technology to emerge from electronic trial has been real-time transcript:

> '[T]he ability of the court reporter to use a computer-assisted stenograph machine and have the testimony of a witness appear on the computer monitor in plain English text within a matter of seconds from the time when the words were spoken'.[21]

It greatly increases the immediacy and accessibility of transcript, eliminating the need for the judge to make notes during the trial.[22]

---

[19] See information at <http://www.vcat.vic.gov.au/vcat_online/vcat_online.htm>.

[20] Leeuwenburg and Wallace, *above* n. 4, 8-9.

[21] Andrews, quoted in Vicki Harris, *Technology for Justice Conference Presentations*, Australian Institute of Judicial Administration, (CD-ROM) (1998). 'The "computer magic" is accomplished by the matching of the reporter's stenographic keystrokes with the same stroking already stored in the reporter's "computer dictionary" and associated with a specific English word. If a "match" does not occur, an "untranslate" appears on the screen in the form of the stenographic keystroke which, of course, are unreadable to the untrained eye but which can later be corrected by the court reporter or his/her assistant or "scopist".' Ibid.

[22] Harris, ibid. Its other advantages include:
- enables the court to refer to the exact wording of a question or statement before making a ruling on an objection;
- assists those who are hard of hearing in court;
- allows court interpreters to refer the monitor during their translation for a witness.

Once the transcript is available in electronic form, technology enables it to be searched, analysed and indexed.[23] Parties and the judge can have the ability to annotate their own copies of the transcript.

While the benefits of real-time transcripts may be most particularly felt in long or complex trials,[24] discussion with judges and counsel suggest that it is rapidly gaining popularity in all types of cases. The factor impeding its more widespread use is its cost, in particular, the cost associated with having highly trained court operators to 'translate' the spoken word to text.

However, we are moving towards a situation where transcript can be produced without having an operator in the courtroom. The use of digital video recordings for transcript is already possible in many courts. The use of integrated audio and video technology and improved voice recognition software are close to reality.[25]

Consequent cost reductions are likely to see this technology more widely available, as is already happening overseas.[26] The future may see the evolution of a multi-media court record, in which the court can select between real-time stenographic transcript, audio, video recording, or a combination of them, according to the requirements of the case.[27]

Once transcript is available in electronic form, it can also be made available faster to parties outside courtroom hours, via e-mail delivery. The Victorian Government Reporting Service now uses e-mail as its preferred form of delivery for transcript and, in that state, transcript can be prepared from an audio recording transmitted from a remote location and e-mailed back to that location the same day.[28]

---

[23] Harris, *above* n. 21.

[24] Robert Cock QC, 'Evidentiary Rules and Aids In The Presentation Of Evidence' (Paper presented to the Criminal Trial Reform Conference, Melbourne, 24-25 March 2000), at <http://www.aija.org.au/ctr/COCK.HTM>.

[25] Victorian Parliamentary Law Reform Committee, *above* n. 6, [10.61-62]. Leeuwenburg and Wallace, *above* n. 4, 21-22.

[26] Leeuwenburg and Wallace, ibid.

[27] April Artegian, 'The Technology-augmented Court Record', Fifth National Court Technology Conference, 9-12 September 1997, National Center for State Courts, (CD-ROM) (1997). See also Lord Chancellor's Department, 'Resolving and Avoiding disputes in the Information Age. A Lord Chancellor's Department Consultation Paper', September 1998, <http://www.open.gov.uk/lcd/consult/itstrat/civcon.htm>.

[28] Writer's conversation with Mick Francis at VGRS, 20 July 2001.

Technology can also enable a running transcript to be provided outside the physical environment of the courtroom. This can be done via an Intranet available only to the parties. It is also possible to make the transcript publicly available on an Internet web site.

2.2.6   Video conferencing/Cybercourts

Video conferencing is now widely available in court proceedings and Australian courts have largely taken the lead in exploring new uses for it.[29] This is perhaps a product of the enormous distances which courts have to cover, particularly in the larger states. It is used to take evidence from overseas, from a witness or party in custody, to hear expert evidence, as an alternative to circuit hearings, to conduct directions hearings or pre-trial conferences, to hear chamber applications, for appeal hearings, for applications for special leave in the High Court, to hand down judgements, to conduct remands and even, on occasion, to pass sentence.[30]

The technology itself has become cheaper and more available and protocols for linking different brands of equipment have improved. More familiarity with the technology has resulted in cheaper and more efficient set up. Nevertheless some barriers remain. These include the cost of the ISDN line connections, the need to locate a video conferencing facility in a specific location and some of the distractions associated with variable picture quality and set up.[31]

---

[29] Martin Gruen, 'Courtroom Audio, Video, and Videoconferencing', Fifth National Court Technology Conference, 9-12 September 1997, National Center for State Courts, (CD-ROM) (1997).

[30] The Hon Daryl Williams, 'Address to the Australian Institute of Judicial Administration Technology for Justice Conference', *Technology for Justice Conference Presentations,* Australian Institute of Judicial Administration (CD-ROM) (1998); Practice Note No. 2 of 1998 issued under Section 42Q of the Evidence Act 1958 (Vic) 'Courts and Tribunals Practice Notes' (May 1998) Vol. 72 No. 5 *Law Institute Journal,* 71; GRD Waldron, DAT Jones, Clive Alsop and Mick Francis, 'Audio visual Technology and Victorian Courts', *Technology for Justice Conference Presentations,* Australian Institute of Judicial Administration (CD-ROM) (1998), Sir Gerard Brennan, 'Opening Address AIJA Technology for Justice Conference Melbourne', *above* n. 1; Australian Law Reform Commission, *above* n. 5, [5.37, 5.39, 5.40-41,5.57]; Leeuwenburg and Wallace, *above* n. 4, 10.

[31] Leeuwenburg and Wallace, *above* n. 4, 10.

Many of these difficulties can be overcome by the use of desktop video conferencing over the Internet. Better compression software, higher bandwidth Internet connections (and the possibility of wireless technology) mean that the future is likely to see greater use this technology to provide courts with great flexibility in terms of the locations from which evidence can be taken by this method.

Although some concerns have been expressed about the use of the technology in terms of its effect on witnesses, the potential for prejudice to a party as a result[32] and possible cost concerns,[33] its use to date does not seem to have given rise to any great objection. However, it has been necessary for courts to clearly control its use and address procedural issues. Guidelines and practice directions, in some cases quite detailed, address issues such as the presence of third parties, provision for confidential communications between an accused and his legal representative, even control of camera viewpoint and audio links.[34]

In the United Kingdom, it has been suggested that video conferencing could replace some of the need for physical courts, providing greater, although perhaps different, access to justice.[35] In theory, the technology exists now to make a 'virtual court' a reality. For example, in Victoria, on at least one occasion, video conferencing technology has been used bring a substitute magistrate 'on-line' to a country court house to overcome difficulties caused by the unanticipated absence of a resident magistrate.[36]

If the judicial officer can participate in that way, why not the jury? The possibility of on-line jury trials has already been identified – one commentator has pointed to the possibility of juries consisting of thousands of people, chosen from electoral rolls and through the Internet, watching the

---

[32] Williams, *above* n. 30. Australian Law Reform Commission, *above* n. 5, [8.28-8.29].

[33] Australian Law Reform Commission, *above* n. 5, [2.40].

[34] See, e.g., Tasmanian Courts 'Video Conferencing Guidelines' at <http://www.courts.tas.gov.au/magistrate/general/videoconf.html#Appearance of other persons by video link> as at 3 May 2001, County Court of Victoria, 'Video Conferencing in the County Court' at <http://www.countycourt.vic.gov.au/vid_conf.htm> as at 3 May 2001 and Northern Territory Courts, 'Videoconferencing Bookings and Procedures' at <http://www.nt.gov.au/ntsc/doc/Videoconf_Policy.doc>.

[35] Lord Chancellor's Department, *above* n. 27.

[36] Author's notes, 'Session Five: Videoconferencing – a Multi-purpose Tool', AIJA Technology for Justice Conference, Melbourne, 23 March 1998.

trial on Internet enabled web TV. While this may sound far-fetched, in fact all the technology to make it possible exists now.[37]

The issue is not the technology, but the choices that we make about the way we use it. While experience to date suggests that courts and counsel have been comfortable using technology for aspects of the trial process, the prospect of a trial conducted wholly in cyberspace is perhaps not something that sits comfortably with our notion of the essential nature of a criminal trial. Whether or not that is something that may change in future is open to debate.

2.2.7 Use of technology to assist the jury

The jury is one of the essential elements of the criminal trial process in Australia's higher and intermediate courts. The desire to assist the jury to understand the evidence presented to them has been one of the significant factors compelling the use of technology, particularly in complex trials involving detailed documentary evidence.

The facilities of the electronic courtroom make it possible for courts to think in positive terms about the ways in which technology may be of assistance to the jury in a particular case. Quite recently, a number of judges have begun to take quite an active role in considering the needs of the jury in this regard.

In one complex fraud trial recently,[38] the judge considered the question of assistance for the jury at the outset of the trial and discussed the matter with counsel. Inquiries were made of the jury as to both their degree of computer literacy and the type of assistance they would find useful. One possible concern was that jurors who were more IT literate might come to dominate proceedings in such an environment.[39] In the event, that did not

---

[37] Tony Sutherland, 'The Internet and Beyond: A New Order for Justice?' (Paper delivered to the AIJA Technology for Justice Conference, Melbourne, 9 October 2000), AIJA (2001) CD-ROM; see also at <http://www.aija.org.au/tech2/present.htm#sutherland>.

[38] *R v. Bruce Ivar Dowding, Bruno Gordano Grollo, Rino John Grollo*, Supreme Court of Victoria, No. 1420 of 1999. Details provided by author's interview with Justice Bernard Teague, Supreme Court of Victoria, 10 April 2001.

[39] It should be noted however, that imbalances can arise on juries in other ways, e.g., the note taker often assumes a disproportionate amount of influence because of their status as 'custodian of the record'.

emerge as an issue in that case, as the foreman advised that the majority of the jury were computer literate and that they wanted computer assistance.

As a result, the jury was given access to two stand-alone computers, secured in the jury room. Each had access to word processing, imaged copies of documentary exhibits and electronic transcript. For note-taking purposes, the jurors were provided access to word processing software with each juror's notes protected by their own password.

To provide transcript to the jury, it was necessary for the judge to settle a version of transcript that did not contain parts of the transcript that the jury should not see, for example, argument conducted in their absence. An arrangement was devised whereby parties advised the judge's associate by e-mail of corrections and amendments. This is an example of a standard, readily available and low-cost technology, put to an effective use in the trial process.

The assistance provided to the jury in that case was prompted by consideration of the recommendations of a recent report by the New Zealand Law Reform Commission, which found that significant number of jurors have difficulty in concentrating upon, assimilating and recalling evidence presented by way of oral testimony. It was suggested that part of the solution, may lie in the greater use of both written and visual aids in their opening and closing addresses and in evidence-in-chief and that there may be a role for the appropriate use of technology in that.[40]

That technology does not need to be confined to the use of the types of specialist systems used in complex trials. Most personal computers come equipped with a number of standard office technology tools. Once a courtroom is equipped with a basic technology infrastructure, there is little additional cost involved in using these tools and they can be put to some very effective uses.

One of the most common is Microsoft PowerPoint. A number of Australian judges have begun to experiment with PowerPoint slides as part of

---

[40] Warren Young, Neil Cameron and Yvette Tinsley, *Juries in Criminal Trials Part Two: A Summary of Research Findings*, Preliminary paper 37 No. 2, New Zealand Law Commission, November 1999 at <http://www.lawcom.govt.nz/documents/publications/ PP37Vol2.pdf> as at 4 April 2001, chapter 3, 'The Trial Process'; Law Commission of New Zealand, *Juries in Criminal Trials*, Report 69, February 2001 at <http://www. lawcom.govt.nz/documents/publications/r69.PDF> [356-9].

their directions to the jury. A presentation by one of the those judges at the AIJA's *Technology for Justice Conference* last October, focussed in some detail on a number of the issues which judges need to consider in adapting such technology for use in the courtroom, in particular, the principles used in determining the content and format of such presentations. The approach has been well received and appears to offer advantages in terms of clarity, keeping jurors' attention and reducing the number of requests for clarification during deliberation.[41]

The use of such tools by counsel needs to be subject to appropriate judicial supervision to ensure that such aids do no more than summarise or collate testimony given under oath, rather than present new evidence.[42]

2.2.8 Public Information

Most courts in Australia now have court web sites which contain a variety of material including information about the court process and what to expect at court, virtual guides to the courtroom, access to court forms, contact details, links to other resources and education material for schools. Several courts have now created areas on their web sites which record judges' comments on passing sentence[43] a system which has proven to be remarkably effective in reducing errors made by the media in reporting cases.[44]

Most of the debate about the use of technology to assist public understanding of the criminal trial process to date has centred on the question of televising court proceedings. That debate, itself, has moved on over the past couple of years as technology has made possible to broadcast live

---

[41] Judge Mary Ann Yeats, 'The Use of Powerpoint in charging Juries' (Paper presented to AIJA Technology for Justice Conference, Melbourne, 8-10 October 2000) at <http://www.aija.org.au/tech2/presentations/yeats/charging.htm>.

[42] Young, et al., *above* n. 40, [3.8].

[43] See, e.g., Supreme Court of the Northern Territory, 'Judge's Comments on Passing Sentence' at <http://www.nt.gov.au/ntsc/remarks.html>, Supreme Court of Tasmania, 'Publication of Sentencing Details on the Internet' at <http://www.courts.tas.gov.au/supreme/sentences/sentintr.html>.

[44] Justice Peter Underwood, Supreme Court of Tasmania, 'Communicating decisions on sentencing to the public via the Internet' (Paper delivered to the AIJA Technology for Justice Conference, Melbourne, 9 October 2000) at <http://www.aija.org.au/tech2/present.htm#underwood>.

sound and vision of court proceedings on the Internet.[45] The Federal Court has used this audio-visual streaming technology to publish 'live' judgements on its web site. The New South Wales Land and Environment Court recently announced plans to make transcripts of its hearings available to the public on the court web site[46] and several recent Royal Commissions have enabled the public to follow proceedings in this way.[47]

In theory, this technology combined with digital audio recording of court proceedings would enable each court to become the electronic broadcaster of its own live court proceedings. The proposition that a court web site might become an extension of the public gallery[48] raises some difficult issues, some of which have already been canvassed in the debates about televising of court proceedings. It has the potential to increase public knowledge and understanding of the work of the courts. However, there are issues about privacy that also need to be carefully considered. How would we feel about the transcript of a rape victim being made available on the Internet?[49] What about the possibility of jurors being able to access portions of proceedings relating to rulings made in their absence? Do courts have to consider differential access rights to some material for parties and the public?

2.2.9 The influence of IT on criminal legislation and legal practice – equity, access and the role of the court

It has recently been suggested that the issue in relation to the use of technology in the courtroom is not so much the availability of the technology, but rather matters such as fairness, social justice and evidentiary issues.[50]

---

[45] Daniel Stepniak and Paul Mason, '"Court in the web" The impact of the Internet on the cameras in court debate' (April 2000) 25(2) *Alternative Law Journal* 71.

[46] Adam Creed, 'Australian State Unveils Online Legal System', 25 April 2001, Newsbytes at <http://www.newsbytes.com/news/01/164944.html>; see also Land and Environment Court web site at <http://www.lawlink.nsw.gov.au/lec.nsf/pages/ecallover>.

[47] Longford Royal Commission web site <http://www.vgrs.vic.gov.au/public/longford.html> as at 24 April 2001, Metropolitan Ambulance Service Royal Commission web site <http://www.masrc.org/> as at 24 April 2001.

[48] Stepniak and Mason, *above* n. 45, 73.

[49] Victorian Parliamentary Law Reform Committee, *above* n. 6, [8.39].

[50] Cock, *above* n. 24.

To that, I would add the issue of 'cultural change', that is, the attitude that both the legal profession and the Judiciary adopt towards the use of new technology and its effect on their work practices.

As far as evidentiary matters are concerned, this topic was the subject of detailed examination by the Queensland Law Reform Commission in 1998 and has also been the subject of recent discussion in other jurisdictions.[51] The use of technology has required adjustments to evidentiary rules and to court rules and practice directions.[52] By and large, however, this has not been controversial. The main challenge is to ensure that the law keeps pace with changes in technology.

However, notwithstanding changes in the law, concerns have also been expressed that 'potential savings in time and costs can be lost if lawyers adopt rigidly adversarial positions, challenge the electronic presentations and require the documents to be dealt with in the old time-consuming way.'[53]

There has been no empirical research conducted on the use of IT in trials, but anecdotal experience suggests that much depends on the attitude of the judge and, perhaps to a lesser extent, the attitude of the prosecutors and defence lawyers. Certainly it is clear that the larger systems that have been developed and worked well have required very close co-operation between the courts and the parties to achieve that result. A judge who is technologically literate and prepared to take the initiative in considering the appropriate use of technology in a particular case can go some way towards persuading counsel who may be unsure or reluctant.

---

[51] Queensland Law Reform Commission, *The Receipt of Evidence by Queensland Courts: Electronic Records*, Issues Paper WP No. 52, August 1998, Queensland Law Reform Commission. See also Cock, *above* n. 24, and Western Australian Law Reform Commission, *Review of the Criminal and Civil Justice System – Final Report*, Chapter 35 'Technology and Justice' at <http://www.wa.gov.au/lrc/finalreport/finalreporthtml/ch35 technology.html>.

[52] See list at <http://www.aija.org.au/info/techn/rules.htm>.

[53] The Hon Daryl Williams, 'White Collar Crime – a Challenge to the Criminal Justice System' (Paper presented to 'Perspectives on White Collar Crime Towards 2000' Seminar, Adelaide, 27 February 1998), 12-13. The Commonwealth Director of Public Prosecutions has referred to the importance of defence co-operation in ensuring the usefulness and effectiveness of an electronic courtroom system; see Brian Martin, 'Prosecution Issues' (Paper presented to 'Perspectives on White Collar Crime Towards 2000' Seminar, Adelaide, 27 February 1998), 6.

However, judges may need to exercise some caution. It is important that technology serves as a tool, rather than a weapon. Courts need to ensure that both parties have equality of access to the technology.

One commentator has observed that there may well be a difference between criminal and civil trials in this respect. In civil cases, the parties may tend to belong to the interactive community of those who are empowered with computer technology. In the criminal trial, on the other hand, there may generally not be equality of power between prosecution and defence with regard to use of technology.

On the prosecution side the use of technology at the case preparation and management level can be intensive. The defence may not be in that position and, for that that reason, there is a need to consider how this impacts on unrepresented or legally-aided accused or even on those accused whose solicitors are unwilling or unable to take hold of the technology which has been thrust upon them. This may involve the provision of assistance by the prosecution in terms of providing training and facilitating access to the technology itself. This may be more difficult to achieve in the case of the unrepresented litigant.[54]

At the end of the day, there may be situations where the court will have to limit the use of technology, in order to ensure that its use does not give one party an advantage over the other.

There is an issue, of course, as to how far this care by the court should go? Does it go as far as safeguarding parties' interests against their (or their lawyers') lack of expertise with technology? Is there an argument that expertise with technology in the courtroom is a professional skill that advocates should be expected to have, or to acquire? On the other hand, could mandating the use of technology (and, in effect, requiring that skill) deprive a party of his or her choice of counsel?

The use of technology also adds another dimension to the role of the court in the pre-trial management phase. Care needs to be exercised to ensure that the technology used by both prosecution and defence is compatible (where a common system is not used). Protocols need to be established for the delivery and management of exhibits and the overall main-

---

[54] Michael Rozenes, 'Session One: Electronic Courts – Session Notes', *Technology for Justice Conference Presentations*, Australian Institute of Judicial Administration (CD-ROM) (1998).

tenance of discipline in the use of systems[55] and, particularly for those participants who may have little existing computer knowledge, there is a need to ensure that sufficient training and technical support is available.

There has been no empirical research done on the effect of the use of technology in relation to work practices. Certainly it appears that these types of cases involve far greater attention at the pre-trial management stage, where technology issues, as well as the general case management issues, have to be factored into the planning process.[56] It would be interesting to know, for example, what are the effects, if any, of having to incorporate requirements imposed by the technology into the case preparation phase on the lawyers' work practices? What implication does the use of technology in the courtroom have for styles of advocacy? What effect does its use have on juries?[57] How does it affect the work of the judge? Research on these areas could, in turn, assist in developing more effective technologies for use in the trial process.

2.2.10   The level of courtroom automation/Infrastructure needs

While there is much that is available, and although Australian courts have in some respects taken a pioneering role in the use of technology, there is still considerable scope for its more widespread and effective use.

Effective use of technology in the trial process depends, firstly, on there being in place, a basic, modern, infrastructure for its use. This applies not only to the physical environment of the courtroom, but to the systems and processes of the court, its administration and case management systems. The last five years have seen considerable efforts in many Australian jurisdictions to install and up-date systems and infrastructure and to introduce technology into the courtroom. However, inability to access the tools offered by technology is still probably the most significant factor inhibiting its more widespread and effective use.

Particularly in the lower end, high volume criminal jurisdiction, the lack of a basic technology infrastructure remains a significant issue and an impediment to the more widespread use of technology.

---

[55] Ibid.

[56] Smith and Chivers, *above* n. 6.

[57] Rozenes, *above* n. 54.

2.2.11   Use of technology/user support

Concerns have been expressed from time to time that the legal profession in Australia has generally been slow to embrace these technologies. It has been suggested that:

> 'To properly harness the technology, ... requires a commitment to training and cultural change. Many investigators and lawyers with require encouragement to abandon paper based work practices and to embrace the opportunities the technology offers'.[58]

The same is true for judges and magistrates. There has been no empirical research done in Australia on the use of technology specific to particular professional groups. However, the latest available statistical information indicates that, during the twelve months to November 2000 9.2 million adults, or 66 per cent of all adults in Australia, used a computer. The incidence of use decreases with age and for the age groups 40-44 and 55+ (the categories in which the majority of serving judicial officers would fall) the percentage of those who accessed a computer at work during that period were 55 per cent and 12 per cent respectively.[59]

In the writer's observations, most judicial officers would fall somewhere on a continuum between those who might be categorised as 'committed and inventive users' and those who have yet to be persuaded that the use of information technology has anything to offer them. That would probably also be true of most lawyers. Experience suggests that the factors that may move people closer to one end of the spectrum than another include access to user-friendly, intuitive technology that is of immediate practical relevance to the task in hand and which is accompanied by high quality, and timely, technical support and training. That training and support needs to recognise the realities associated with workflows in busy courts and accommodate individual work practices.

---

[58] Joseph Longo, 'Investigation Issues' (Paper presented to 'Perspectives on White Collar Crime Towards 2000' Seminar, Adelaide, 27 February 1998), 8.

[59] Australian Bureau of Statistics, '8147.0 Use of the Internet by Householders, Australia', 16 February 2001 at <http://www.abs.gov.au/ausstats/ABS%40.nsf/b06660592430 724fca2568b5007b8619/ae8e67619446db22ca2568a9001393f8!OpenDocument>.

It is perhaps axiomatic to observe that people who have well-established and successful work methods will require to be convinced of the necessity to change those work methods. However, the most successful developments in Information Technology in courts seem to be those that set out to consult with and inform and educate their potential users, rather than those that assume that the benefits of the new system are obvious.

Several courts have issued draft Practice Directions in relation to the use of technology in civil matters during the past few years, to provide assistance to the profession and encourage consideration of the use of technology. There is probably scope to extend those efforts into criminal trials.

2.2.12   Initiation of IT projects

It is clear that most of the difficulties relating to the re-engineering of old systems or implementation of new systems involve planning, project management and cost, rather than the technology itself.[60] There is a need to take a team approach to the development of court systems – ensuring that the Judiciary, court administrators and information technology experts are all involved.

There have been calls for the development of a court-based system for use in criminal trials, that is, a generic system that is not specific to a particular prosecution or investigation agency.[61] While some jurisdictions have moved to establish generic systems,[62] the development of court systems that are not tied to any particular commercial software packages[63] is unlikely. Many courts simply do not have the resources to develop their own systems and make them available to the parties.

---

[60] Leeuwenburg and Wallace, *above* n. 4, 14.

[61] Longo, *above* n. 58, 9.

[62] For example, the Electronic Appeal Book developed by the Supreme Court of Western Australia – see Chief Justice David Malcolm, 'The Western Australian Electronic Appeal Book Project' (Paper delivered to the AIJA Technology for Justice Conference, Melbourne, 9 October 2000) at <http://www.aija.org.au/tech2/presentations/malcolm/CJe-appeal.htm>.

[63] Such as the collaboration between the Victorian Supreme Court and Ringtail solutions in Court 13 – see Supreme Court of Victoria, Media Release, 11 October 1999, 'Restored Supreme Court uses Latest Court Technology' at <http://home.vicnet.net.au/~sclib/media/Cybercb.html>.

The two most recent Australian systems designed for use in criminal trials have both been developed by prosecution agencies. One is a joint Litigation Support System developed jointly by ASIC and the Commonwealth DPP and intended as a standard package for use in Commonwealth criminal trials.[64] It is a robust and pragmatic package, which has been used in over 90 matters since 1999, 11 of which have been completed.[65]

Another inexpensive and simple litigation support system has been developed by the Victorian Office of Public Prosecutions. The Electronic Crayon System is a good example of a tool based on existing computer software, designed to be used by those with minimal computer skill and requiring only a modest amount of training.[66]

Where courts lack resources to design and implement their own systems, 'pilot court' project arrangements with commercial systems developers may be appealing. One Australian court has already entered into such an arrangement. However, the use of systems that are tied to particular commercial service providers can create problems for courts. In particular, the court may find itself under pressure from the software provider to mandate particular court rules or practices that are specific to that software. This may affect the ability of parties to access or use different types of software and, in the longer term, restrict the court's ability to develop and adapt its use of technology.

2.2.13 Common technical standards

One particularly pressing issue for the use of IT in Australian courts generally at the moment, is the lack of a common technical standard to enable data to be transferred 'seamlessly' between courts and between courts and court users. This issue has been recognised largely as a result of a project conducted into the feasibility of electronic appeal books.

In recent years, a number of Australia jurisdictions have conducted electronic appeals whereby the appeal books are presented to the court in

---

[64] Leeuwenburg and Wallace, *above* n. 4, 13.

[65] E-mail from Ms Stela Walker, Deputy Director, Corporate Management, Office of the Commonwealth Director of Public Prosecutions to the author, 23 April 2001.

[66] Melinda Brown, 'Legal technology award winners' (December 2000), *Law Institute of Victoria, News*, No. 12, 3.

electronic form and accessed in court on computer equipment, by the parties and the judge.[67]

The concept has received considerable attention at senior levels of the Judiciary. A 1998 report to the Council of Chief Justices of Australia and New Zealand (CCJ) on the feasibility of the use of electronic appeal books, put forward a prototype electronic appeal book and a detailed series of recommendations designed to make it possible for courts to implement it.[68]

While the project had the appellate stage as its primary focus, much of its attention, necessarily, was focused on the processes at trial level which result in the production of documents that form part of appeal books. A major theme of its recommendations was that for electronic appeals to be viable, the documents (such as originating process, transcript and judgments) should be produced in electronic form in a way that is consistent between and across jurisdictions. This would make it possible, for example, for an indictment and a transcript relating to a matter originating in the Supreme Court of Tasmania to be made available in an electronic appeal book before the High Court, with minimum cost and delay. It has the potential to integrate much of the use of technology across Australia's state and federal jurisdictions, to the benefit of all courts.

At present, much of the source material for the appeal book is not produced in electronic form. Few courts have yet moved to a system of electronic filing and documents that are to be incorporated into an electronic appeal book have to be prepared for entry into an electronic computerised management system in a similar fashion to the preparation of documents in an electronic trial. This can be a time-consuming and costly process and would explain why e-appeals, as is the case with electronic trials, are still being approached very much on a case-by-case basis. They tend to be used only in large civil matters where the costs of the litigation would make the preparation of an electronic appeal book worthwhile.[69]

Their incidence is also unlikely to increase significantly in volume until the recommendations of the CCJ report related to the development of

---

[67] Leeuwenburg and Wallace, *above* n. 4, 6.

[68] Jo Sherman and Allison Stanfield, 'Council of Chief Justices of Australia and New Zealand Electronic Appeals Project – Final Report May 1998' (May 1998) at <http://www.ccj.org/>.

[69] Leeuwenburg and Wallace, *above* n. 4, 6-7.

uniform standards across jurisdictions with regard to the way courts receive, process and issue documentation electronically are addressed. The use of a common technical standard based on Legal XML is currently being investigated in relation to a number of areas, including electronic filing and transcript production.[70]

The use of common technical standards is also under investigation in the development of 'whole of jurisdiction' or 'integrated justice' systems, where a common set of guidelines, or software, and maybe even hardware, is used by police, prosecution, remand centres, courts, prisons, sheriffs, and probation authorities. In theory this would reduce costs and duplicated data entry as a case moves from stage to stage. In practice, while a number of Australian jurisdictions are in the process of developing these systems, none are yet operational. The need for common standards applies not only within jurisdictions, i.e., the various states and territories, but also between State and Federal jurisdictions.

2.2.14 The (mandatory) use of (identical) IT-systems by judges and public prosecutors

This has not emerged as an issue in Australia. There are no mandatory requirements to use IT systems in force in relation to judges and courts have, to date, been quite concerned that their systems are separate from prosecution and defence agencies. This is an issue that will need to be addressed with the development of integrated, or 'whole of system' approaches. This would most likely be done by the use of firewall technology, to ensure that differing information needs (and restrictions) could be properly met.

2.2.15 The drawbacks of introducing IT

While the introduction of Information Technology to courts in Australia seems, generally, to be regarded in a fairly positive light, technological change brings with it a host of issues relating to the development, planning, implementation, cost and changed work practices. Of these, re-

---

[70] See Legal XML web site at <http://www.legalxml.org> for details of work being undertaken by various workgroups in the United States and Australia.

source constraints and the pressure placed on limited court budgets by the demands of new technology, are probably the most significant concerns.

2.3   (LEGAL) INFORMATION/KNOWLEDGE MANAGEMENT: THE MOST PRESSING ISSUES

2.3.1   Developments in legal information/knowledge systems

The two significant applications in this area for courts have been case management systems and judicial support systems.

2.3.2   Case Management

The trial process starts long before a case reaches the courtroom and technology has a role to play from an early stage. For over two decades, Australian courts, taking the lead from their counterparts in the United States, have looked to computerised case management systems to more effectively track and manage the progress of cases.

Well-designed, integrated case management systems have the potential to enhance the efficient administration of justice, by facilitating the allocation of resources, scheduling judges' workloads, time-tabling and listing cases and allocating courtrooms.[71] They can also ensure that case information is processed with maximum efficiency, available when and where it is needed and processed in ways and in forms that make it accessible to those who need it.

There is a recognised need for Australian courts to re-engineer case management systems, many are still operating on legacy systems which provide insufficient flexibility and functionality for modern requirements. A number of courts have begun to move in that direction over the past two years, but this remains a significant issue, particularly in courts of summary jurisdiction which tend to have less resources and higher caseloads.

---

[71] Victorian Parliamentary Law Reform Committee, *above* n. 6, [9.5].

There is no common standard or technical specification for case management systems in Australia and this can cause difficulties in terms of system compatibility and comparability of statistical information.

2.3.3 Judicial Support Systems

In this area, one of the most important applications has been the development of specialised judicial support packages to provide access, usually over a court Intranet, to primary research materials, such as cases and legislation, augmented by a variety of other material including sentencing information, bench books and other publications, such as court bulletins or administrative circulars.

One example is the Sentencing Information System (SIS) developed by the Judicial Commission of New South Wales,[72] a computerised sentencing database which is regarded as a world leader in its field. Fast and efficient access to up-to-date information about sentencing decisions is obviously a great assistance to individual judicial officers and clearly helps to promote consistency in sentencing.

Systems available in courts vary considerably in their levels of sophistication, those such as SIS and JIRS in South Australia, which provide an extensive range of materials to courts that still struggle to provide access to electronic databases of their previous decisions.

2.3.4 Use of legal information/knowledge systems

While there has been no empirical research done, it would seem that the use of judicial support and case management systems has increased exponentially over the last decade as their availability has become more widespread.

Some courts have required judicial officers to directly enter data, e.g., court orders, into screens in the courtroom.

---

[72] See Ernest Schmatt, 'The Role & Functions of the Judicial Commission of New South Wales' (Paper delivered at the Judicial Conduct & Ethics Committee Conference, Dublin, Ireland, 6 May 2000) at <http://www.judcom.nsw.gov.au/dublin.htm> as at 3 May 2001.

As familiarity with the technological tools has increased, some magistrates have even developed their own support systems, both for themselves and their colleagues.[73]

Judges and magistrates do require training and assistance in operating these systems. As noted above, that training needs to be provided in ways that recognise the realities of their work practices and their workload.

2.3.5   Use of information/knowledge departments

The use of specialist information/knowledge departments, designated as such, is not common in the courts and agencies working in the legal arena, except for large law firms and some of the larger courts.

In courts, the 'process' type of information is likely to be managed and distributed by the management, and made available to other users as required, via the case management or practice management system.

Management of primary and secondary research materials is largely vested in the library and librarians, whose functions have expanded considerably over the last decade to encompass much of the management and distribution of these types of resources. Judicial Support Systems tend to be run from within the court library (other than in the State of New South Wales, where the system has been developed and managed by that state's Judicial Commission).

2.3.6   Use of statistical information

Case Management systems do now provide better data on the work of criminal courts. The Australian Bureau of Statistics' national criminal courts statistics project aims to harmonise the statistical measures used in the various court systems. It regularly produces national case-flow data showing the number of defendants processed by the higher (Supreme and

---

[73] See, e.g., presentation by South Australian magistrate, Roseanne McInnes SM, 'Bordertown and the Globalisation of Justice', AIJA Technology for Justice Conference, Melbourne, 23 March 1998 at <http://www.aija.org.au/conference98/rmcinn/bordertown idx.htm>; and presentation by another South Australian magistrate, Tony Newman, AIJA Technology for Justice Conference, Melbourne, 9 October 2000 at <http://www.aija. org.au/tech2/presentations/newman/weaving_your_own_web.htm>.

Intermediate) criminal courts. Information is presented for each State or Territory (including the aggregate total for Australia) and for each court level (including the aggregate total for higher courts combined).

The major obstacles to the more efficient collection of data remain the lack of consistent statistical definitions between jurisdictions and the capacities of individual court case management systems. Work is now underway at a co-operative state and federal level to develop a harmonised set of statistical measures for both civil and criminal work.

2.4 THE BENEFICIAL EFFECTS OF THESE DISCUSSIONS

I can really only comment on this from an Australian perspective. In this country, it has been found that it is of considerable assistance to all those involved in developing, applying and studying the use of IT in the court process generally, to have the opportunity to regularly exchange information, ideas and experience. The Australian Institute of Judicial Administration runs a biennial *Technology for Justice Conference* which aims to showcase current developments and issues in the use of IT in the justice system. It is extremely well-supported and part of the lead-up to that event consists of a review of the use of IT in Australian courts and justice agencies.

We have also found considerable benefit in regular contact and information exchange with courts and agencies in our neighbouring countries within the Asia-Pacific region and further afield. Australian courts regularly look to programs run by the US National Center for State Courts in the area of court IT, for a wider perspective on our work.

While there is obviously great potential to exchange information electronically and to use the resources of the Internet to extend the communication possibilities of e-mail, our experience is that face to face discussions and interaction do provide an important opportunity to explore issues in more depth.

Chapter 3
SINGAPORE

Thian Yee Sze

3.1   INTRODUCTION

The use of technology in the Singapore courts has made a key contribution towards building up an institution in the administration of justice which is widely acknowledged as world-class and a first amongst equals.[1]

This article chronicles the Supreme Court's journey in harnessing technology over the past twelve years as we pursued our vision to transform an outdated judicial system into a modern and dynamic pillar of justice which has earned the trust of the society it serves and the confidence of the international business community.[2] It discusses the *raison d'être* behind the decision to put in extensive resources in the use of technology, the systematic and total approach in the implementation of technological initiatives as we moved towards a paperless courtroom, and the birth of the cyber-court. It is hoped that from this article, the reader will be able to appreciate that technology is but a means for fulfilling the age-old duty of delivering justice to the people.

---

[1] See, e.g., Karen Blochlinger, *Primus Inter Pares: Is the Singapore Judiciary First Among Equals*, Vol. 9, No. 3, Pacific Rim Law & Policy Journal (September 2000).

[2] The more pertinent publications and international surveys include: (1) *Business Environment Report 2001*, Political & Economic Risk Consultancy Ltd (PERC) (April 2001); (2) *The Global Competitiveness Report 1998–2001*, World Economic Forum; (3) *The World Competitiveness Yearbook 1998–2001*, IMD International; (4) *Comparative Country Risk Report 2000*, Political & Economic Risk Consultancy Ltd (PERC), 2001 Index of Economic Freedom, The Heritage Foundation and The Wall Street Journal; (5) *The Asia Pacfic Legal 500 – The Guide to Asia's Commercial Law Firms*, 1999; (6) *'Corruption In Asia'*, Asian Intelligence (Issue 507), Wednesday, 1 April 1998; (7) *'Asian Legal System Inadequacies'*, Asian Intelligence (Issue 585), Wednesday, 30 May 2001.

A. Oskamp, et al. (Eds), IT Support of the Judiciary
© *2004, ITeR, The Hague, and the authors*

3.2   Singapore's legal system and judicial structure

Singapore was founded by Sir Thomas Stamford Raffles in 1819 and was a British colony until 1958 when the British Parliament passed the State of Singapore Act which effectively converted the colony into a self-governing state. In 1963, Singapore became part of the Federation of Malaysia. Upon cessation from Malaysia, she became an independent state on 9 August 1965.[3] By virtue of her British colonial roots, Singapore has inherited a rich common law tradition. Singapore has also inherited the adversarial court system from the United Kingdom where the judge does not play an active role in the proceedings before him, unlike in the inquisitorial system in continental Europe where the judge plays a more investigative role. However, we have moved away from the strict adversarial approach in the courtroom. The judge now takes a very proactive approach in the conduct of proceedings in his or her courtroom. Effective trial management has crafted the way in which the advocacy process in court is played out.

Unlike the United Kingdom, Singapore has a written Constitution which sets out, amongst other things, the fundamental liberties accorded to every citizen, and the organisation and functions of the executive, the legislature and the Judiciary in accordance with the Westminster model of government.[4] The Constitution is the supreme law of the land. The two primary sources of law are case law and statutes passed by Parliament.

The constitution and powers of the Judiciary are set out in three main pieces of legislation.[5] Under Article 93 of the Constitution, judicial power is vested in the Supreme Court and in such subordinate courts as may be provided for by any written law. The Supreme Court[6] comprises the

---

[3] For a detailed historical account leading up to Singapore's independence, see Kevin YL Tan, *The Singapore Legal System* (2nd Edition), Singapore University Press (1999).

[4] The Constitution of the Republic of Singapore (1999 Ed). See in particular Parts IV, V, VI and VIII.

[5] The Constitution of the Republic of Singapore, The Supreme Court of Judicature Act (Cap 322) and The Subordinate Courts Act (Cap 321). These are supplemented by secondary legislation such as the Rules of Court, Practice Directions and Registrars' Circulars.

[6] As at 30 April 2002, there are 14 Judges and Judicial Commissioners in the Supreme Court, headed by the Honourable Chief Justice Yong Pung How.

Court of Appeal and the High Court, and hears both civil and criminal matters. The Court of Appeal consists of the Chief Justice, who is also the President of the Court of Appeal, and Judges of Appeal. Judges of the High Court may, at the request of the Chief Justice, sit on the Court of Appeal from time to time. The Court of Appeal became Singapore's final court of appeal on 8 April 1994, when appeals to the Judicial Committee of the Privy Council were abolished. It hears both criminal and civil appeals from decisions of the High Court. The High Court consists of the Chief Justice, Judges and Judicial Commissioners. It hears both criminal and civil cases as a court of first instance and also has appellate jurisdiction over the lower courts.

The Judiciary and the Attorney-General are separate organs of state. They are independent of the executive and the legislature. In contrast, in the United Kingdom, for example, the Lord Chancellor is the head of the Judiciary and is also a member of the Cabinet.

3.3 THE IMPETUS BEHIND THE USE OF TECHNOLOGY

By the end of the 1980s, the state of affairs of the Judiciary was a dismal one. Being an adversarial system, lawyers were expected to act in the interest of their clients by complying with the Rules of Court, and thereby progress their cases towards trial. The reality, however, was contrary to expectations. There were thousands of cases which were clogged up in the court system, some of them for ten years or more. The Rules of Court were breached and totally disregarded. Trials were vacated freely. Trial dates for many cases were three years ahead or more. We had an inefficient Judiciary, which was fuelled by the *laissez faire* attitude of the Bench and the Bar. As one can imagine, the effects of an inefficient Judiciary were detrimental. Public confidence in the Judiciary as the protector of justice was undermined. Many were discouraged from using the litigation process to seek redress for their disputes as it took far too long to have them resolved, if at all. Access to the courts was in effect prevented. As the saying goes – justice delayed is justice denied!

A related problem was access to case-related information both within and outside the Judiciary. For decades, lawyers or members of the public who needed to search for case-related information had to come down personally to the court to plough through piles and piles of cause books and case files to find the relevant information. This was time-consuming and tedious. A search on the status of a company in a winding-up petition could, for instance, take a few days or in some cases, even weeks. Case-related information and statistics were neither comprehensive nor systematic.

When the Honourable Chief Justice Yong Pung How was appointed the head of the Judiciary in September 1990, his singular and paramount mission was to reorganise the Judiciary from top down. At that time, the most pressing concern was the massive backlog of cases which had accumulated, some from the early 1980s. Many initiatives were introduced to tackle this problem, including the reform of archaic procedural rules, the lengthening of court hearing hours, the appointment of more Judges and Judicial Commissioners, the setting up of night courts in the Subordinate Courts and the appointment of Justices' Law Clerks to assist the judges in their legal research.

The key 'weapon' adopted in clearing the backlog of cases was case management. Case management involves the monitoring and managing of cases in the court docket from the time the action is filed to the moment it is finally disposed of by way of a trial, settlement or otherwise. It ensures that all cases progress swiftly without unnecessary delay. All actions are vigilantly monitored. No action is allowed to remain inactive or to 'go to sleep'. With case management, the pace of litigation is controlled by the courts and not the lawyers or the parties.

At that time, an impediment to the effective tracking of the thousands of cases was the non-existence of key information on cases and caseload. We could not easily determine the efficiency of the court system. This provided the impetus for an overhaul of how the courts recorded, kept and archived all such information to make it more easily accessible. As mentioned, case information was recorded in huge cause books which did not have a sensible or simple means of allowing anybody to search for information or obtain vital data and statistics. There was no useful database if one wanted to search for crucial case and other court-related information. It was the urgent need to develop an effective case management regime which gave rise to the genesis of the use of technology in the Judiciary.

3.4 THE EARLY YEARS OF HARNESSING TECHNOLOGY IN THE SUPREME COURT

A computerised case management system known as the Civil System was developed. It is a simple and practical Main Frame system[7] which contains virtually all the important information and statistics of every action, cause or matter filed in court, including the parties' particulars, the nature and quantum of the claim, the documents filed and the outcome of hearings. The computerised Civil System aids in the tracking of a case during its life-cycle. If it becomes inactive or if there is a default by the parties in the compliance with a court order, the system is able to automatically detect such cases. Notices will then be sent to the parties' counsel for them to come and attend before the court so that such lapses in the progression of the case can be rectified. The Civil System ensures that every case is put through the strict case management practice laid down by the courts. The development of the Civil System has played a critical role in the overwhelming success of case management. There is no more backlog in the court system. Almost all cases are disposed of within a year of the commencement of the action, and within six months in the majority of cases.

The Civil System contains the database which is the source of information for many of the information search services on LawNet.[8] The Civil System contains detailed information on all classes of actions in the courts, including writ of summons actions, originating summons, bankruptcy, companies winding up, admiralty and probate. Lawyers, businessmen, creditors and bank officers processing loans are able to do on-line searches on the database through LawNet to obtain the relevant information. Court awards in taxation of costs and assessment of damages in personal injury cases are stored in the Civil System, and provide a very convenient way for judges, judicial officers and lawyers alike who need to look up case precedents.

---

[7] The antiquated Mainframe Civil System will be migrated onto the Electronic Filing System platform in Phase 5 of the Electronic Filing System project (the targeted date of implementation is the 4th quarter 2002/1st quarter 2003).

[8] A detailed discussion on LawNet is found at p. 63.

3.5   The vision of a paperless courtroom – towards building up a world-class Judiciary

By the mid-1990s, the entire backlog of cases in the court docket was cleared as a result of the rigorous case management strategy, aided by computerisation. The initial success which the Supreme Court had with the use of technology in improving the workings of the court reinforced the notion that technology, harnessed with purpose and innovation, could be instrumental in building up a first-rate Judiciary. It was this belief that sowed the seed for a vision of a paperless courtroom.

What are the elements of a world-class Judiciary? It is submitted that first and foremost, it should have high-quality and progressive judges with a solid grasp of the law and a sharp, analytical mind. Secondly, the institutional set-up supporting the judges should be efficient and effective. Thirdly, a world-class Judiciary must be dynamic and able to quickly evolve in order to meet the rapidly changing needs of society.

The use of technology has been a cornerstone in the Singapore Judiciary's goal of developing a world-class Judiciary. After careful study and analysis, it was decided that court processes had to be converted from an arduous paper regime to a streamlined electronic one. This would enhance the efficiency and effectiveness of the courts.

A paperless court system requires the computerisation of every court process, from the filing of court documents to legal research in the preparation of cases by counsel to the trial before the judge. The planning, development and implementation of all key technological initiatives in the Supreme Court over the past few years has made the vision of a paperless courtroom a reality. These technological initiatives have culminated in a total and integrated Electronic Litigation System.

3.6   An Electronic Litigation System for the 21st century

What proves to be the greatest challenge in introducing any technological initiative in a profession steeped in tradition is to change the mindset of its members. During the planning stage for an Electronic Litigation System, the leadership was alive to the fact that a critical factor for success was the acceptance by the judges and lawyers of the revolutionary mode of conducting the litigation process in an entirely paperless or electronic environment. It was understandable that there would be resistance from the ground, especially since most members of the profession were brought up and worked in a setting in which paper was part of their everyday lives. With this concern in mind, the leadership made sure that there would be sufficient time for the members of the legal profession to adjust to working in an electronic environment before a large-scale implementation of any technological initiative.

Detailed planning began in the early 1990s. Six rudiments of the litigation process were identified as the crucial drivers in this ambitious Electronic Litigation System project:

- conduct of trials and hearings;
- filing of court documents;
- access to court information;
- service of court documents;
- legal research;
- internal court processes.

In order to have a totally electronic litigation system, all six rudiments of the litigation process had to be computerised. This entailed having an electronic litigation process from the inception of the case to its final disposal. This was not an easy feat to accomplish, since all the processes in the litigation cycle were entirely paper-based. All court documents were filed in paper. Trials and hearings were conducted with the judge, the lawyer and the witness referring to paper documents. During the planning process, numerous considerations in this regard were taken into account. We had to look into the electronic filing, processing, storage and retrieval of court documents. Trials and hearings would have to be conducted in an electronic environment using electronic documents. This in turn meant that courtrooms and chambers in which hearings were conducted had to be equipped with the necessary physical infrastructure to support electronic hearings. The paperless system would be incomplete without adequate legal research facilities available on-line. Without this, one would have to spend hours ploughing through thick volumes of law reports and other legal authorities in the library. The pursuit of an Electronic Litigation System led to the development and implementation of several innovative technological initiatives in the Supreme Court.

3.7   ELECTRONIC TRIALS AND HEARINGS – THE BIRTH OF THE TECHNOLOGY COURTS

The 'hardware' or the physical infrastructure to support litigation in an electronic environment had to be in place. In the course of planning, it was realised that in order to develop a judicial system which is of high efficiency and quality, a courtroom which would allow lawyers to present their cases more effectively and succinctly, harnessing the full benefits of technology towards this end needed to be constructed. It was likewise critical that judges and lawyers would be comfortable with conducting trials and hearings in an electronic environment. By 1994, the blueprint for a technology court was mapped. A technology court would allow judges and lawyers to experience the use of technology in the courtroom and hopefully, come to appreciate the advantages which technology can bring in the conduct of cases. The first technology court was completed in July 1995. It was a prototype courtroom of the future. It housed advanced technologies such as video conferencing and other audio-visual facilities, and a digital recording system. This gave the legal profession an insight of what was to come in the use of court technology and an opportunity to be exposed to presenting cases with the aid of computers. Numerous cases have been heard in Technology Court 1. The success of the first technology court prompted the construction of a second technology court, which was designed incorporating feedback from judges and practitioners. In the construction of Technology Court 2, a conscious effort was made to retain the original architectural design and flavour of the neo-classical courtroom. With its various technological features, the courtroom improves the quality in the presentation of cases and makes the taking of evidence from witnesses more effective. The main features of Technology Court 2 enhance four key areas of the court's functions – control of court proceedings, presentation of evidence, recording of proceedings and taking of evidence by way of video conferencing.

The court officer is able to control a wide range of functions in the courtroom by using a colour touch-screen panel. He is able to control the audio and lighting levels in the courtroom. He is also able to control all eight cameras located in the room to pan across the courtroom or zoom in on a particular corner. The recording systems, telephone and video conferencing facilities are also activated using this touch-screen panel.

The presentation of cases and the taking of evidence from witnesses are made easier and more effective. For instance, the audiovisual system allows evidence stored in a wide variety of media, including digital video discs and video compact discs, to be tendered to court and viewed from a 100-inch projection screen. The video projection system is capable of projecting images from many sources, for example, the cameras in the courtroom, the video conferencing system and notebook computers. Power outlets and telephone ports have also been installed for the convenience of lawyers and the press. Lawyers can use their laptops in the presentation of evidence. Video content and computer animation can be incorporated to enhance the presentation of technically complex cases. This is especially useful in, say, patent infringement and ship collision cases. As the saying goes, a picture paints a thousand words. It is easier and more effective to describe, for example, how a particular machine works by playing a video of the running of the machine instead of attempting to describe it in words. A popular facility in the technology court is video conferencing.[9] It is a useful means for a witness to give evidence if he or she is not able to be physically present in court for one reason or another. In this way, evidence may be taken from anywhere in the world. It also saves time and costs. There is no need for foreign witnesses to be flown all the way to Singapore, which is both time-consuming and costly.

The use of the technology courts brings with it many advantages. First and foremost, it presents more effective methods for counsel's presentation of cases. There is efficient control of court proceedings by the court officer with a single control panel. There is added convenience for the lawyers, who are able to dial up to their office servers or the Internet for on-line research from their laptops. Members of the press can e-mail stories back to their headquarters immediately. The technology courts symbolise Singapore's model courtroom in the 21st century.

---

[9] Video conferencing sessions have been conducted with witnesses from the USA, the United Kingdom, Switzerland, the Netherlands, Australia, Belgium, Italy and Japan, among other countries.

3.8   USE OF ELECTRONIC DOCUMENTS IN THE COURTROOM

Another milestone in the Electronic Litigation System project was the pilot phase of the use of electronic documents in the courtroom. From August 1998, all appeals before the Court of Appeal and magistrate's appeals in criminal matters before the Chief Justice were heard using electronic documents. The decision to introduce the use of electronic documents in the highest courts of the land was strategically timed. First, the compulsory implementation of the electronic filing of documents and hearings was in the horizon (in 2000). Judges and lawyers would have more than a year's exposure to this novel method of hearing. This would ease them into working in an electronic environment. Secondly, by introducing electronic documents in hearings before the most senior judges who sat at the apex of the Judiciary, a strong message would be sent to the legal profession as to the importance and seriousness which the Judiciary, from top down, placed on the use of technology to better the litigation process. The Judiciary was leading this e-revolution from the front. It was also hoped that when the lawyers witnessed even the most senior judges making the effort to learn how to use computers in their work, they would be encouraged to follow suit and feel less daunted.

Towards this end, the Court of Appeal and the Chief Justice's court (Court No. 1) was renovated and retrofitted with raised flooring to run cables and wires, computer terminals with flat screen monitors, video switching devices for communication between the judge and counsel and customised lecterns. Numerous demonstrations and presentations were conducted for the legal profession. Courtrooms were opened up to allow lawyers ample opportunities to have hands-on practice in handling electronic documents. Specially trained court officers assisted counsel both at practice sessions and during hearings.

Slowly but surely, judges and lawyers grew accustomed to using electronic documents and became adept at accessing, reading and annotating electronic documents. All the courtrooms in the Supreme Court were eventually equipped to handle electronic documents during hearings. In October 1999, the use of electronic documents was extended to all criminal trials and selected civil trials.

With the success of the use of the technology courts and electronic documents, the foundation had been firmly established for the impending implementation of the Electronic Filing System – the pivotal technological initiative which has converted the entire litigation landscape from one likened to a 'paper mountain' to an 'electronic super-highway'.

3.9   THE ELECTRONIC FILING SYSTEM[10] – A LITIGATION SYSTEM *PAR EXCELLENCE*

With the click of a mouse, the Electronic Filing System has changed forever the way court documents are filed, served, processed, stored, retrieved and managed, and the environment in which court proceedings are conducted.

3.9.1   The four services of the Electronic Filing System

The Electronic Filing System fully exploits the electronic highway to minimise the physical movement of people and paper documents. Many of the transactions which used to require visits to the court premises or law firms have been replaced by transactions conducted through computers over the Internet. The criticality of the Electronic Fling System in the Judiciary's pursuit of an Electronic Litigation System cannot be underestimated as its impact cuts across all six rudiments of the litigation process identified above through the four services it provides:

• Electronic Filing Service;
• Electronic Extracts Service;
• Electronic Service of Documents Facility;
• Electronic Information Service.

Electronic Filing Service
Traditionally, documents are filed in court manually over the court registry counter in paper form. Law firms engage court clerks to make daily trips to the registry to do the filing. The Electronic Filing Service allows lawyers to file all documents electronically via the web-based front-end system, which was launched in July 2001. For law firms with the neces-

---

[10] See <http://www.efs.com.sg>.

sary computer equipment, they are able to perform the filing from the convenience of their office or anywhere else in the world. Presently, over 80 per cent of documents are filed in court electronically by more than 300 law firms via the web-based system. More than 750,000 court documents have been electronically filed to date. On average, 2,000 documents are processed electronically on a daily basis.[11] For law firms or litigants-in-person who do not have these computer facilities, two Service Bureaux have been set up, one in the Supreme Court and the other in the Subordinate Courts, to process paper submissions and assist in the electronic filing of documents upon the payment of a manual handling fee.

Electronic Extracts Service
The second service is the Electronic Extracts Service. Under the paper regime, extracts of documents filed in court are obtained by first applying by way of a praecipe (or request) for the documents to be inspected, and then obtaining the extracts in paper copy over the court registry counter. The Electronic Extracts Service allows the process of seeking approval and extraction of copies of cause papers from the court to be done electronically from the lawyer's office or via the Service Bureau. The service is offered in two ways. First, lawyers can make on-line searches on the index of documents filed for a case. Secondly, lawyers can have electronic copies of documents 'e-mailed' to them.

Electronic Service of Documents Facility
The third service is the Electronic Service of Documents Facility. As its name implies, this allows law firms to serve court documents on other law firms electronically, one or more of them concurrently by one click of the mouse. The documents to be served are 'mailed' electronically to the other law firm, in the same way that documents are 'mailed' electronically to court under the Electronic Filing Service. Documents which are served using the Electronic Service of Documents Facility are deemed to be effectively served in compliance with the Rules of Court. A certificate of service is automatically generated by the system. This certificate can be filed in court in lieu of the affidavit of service as evidence of service. The service facility is not only more convenient for the lawyers but

---

[11] Figures are accurate as of 31 March 2002.

also leads to savings in manpower costs as despatch clerks need not be hired to go from place to place to serve court documents personally.

Electronic Information Service
The fourth service is the Electronic Information Service. With this, law firms can perform search queries on the courts' databases electronically from their offices or at the Service Bureau. It encompasses all the LawNet search services.

3.9.2 The six components of the Electronic Filing System

The Electronic Filing System comprises six main components. They are:

- Web-based Law Firm Front-End System;
- VAN Operator Filing Processing System;
- Service Bureau System;
- Courts Workflow System;
- Key Management System;
- Commissioner for Oaths System.

Web-based Law Firm Front-End System
The Web-based Law Firm Front-End System enables law firms to prepare their court documents on their personal computers and subsequently electronically file them to the courts via the Internet. This system also enables law firms to receive information on the outcome of their submissions, as well as extract copies of cause papers from the courts. In addition to the filing of electronic documents to the courts, law firms can serve court documents on other law firms via the Internet through the Front-End System.

VAN Operator Filing Processing System
This system comprises the routing and billing applications. It effectively serves as an electronic post office. Documents received from law firms are opened to check for addresses and other relevant information. The information is then used to route the document to the appropriate court or other recipients. It is also used for the determination of the charges for the transmission or transaction, for example, court fees, processing fees and

hearing fees. In addition, the system handles the collection of monies from the law firms on behalf of the Judiciary.

Service Bureau System

Some law firms do not do much litigation work and, as such, do not subscribe as a registered user of the Electronic Filing System. Some of the litigants may also be acting in person. To cater for such situations, two Service Bureaux have been set up to process paper submissions and to assist in the electronic filing of documents. One is located at the City Hall Building in the Supreme Court. The other is at the Apollo Centre in the Subordinate Courts. The staff at the Bureaux will type in the necessary information, scan the documents to be filed, if required, and transmit the documents electronically to the courts.

Courts Workflow System

The Courts Workflow System is designed to facilitate the tracking and management of cases and documents received by the courts. All documents received are routed to the counter clerk for verification. Once a document is accepted, it may be routed to the appropriate judicial officer for approval. The system also provides case-tracking features. Law firms will be notified of the status of the submission. All approved documents are indexed and stored in the system and access will be given to the electronic case files during hearings and for other purposes as the need may arise. The relevant data is extracted automatically from the documents and used to update the courts' computer databases.

Key Management System

The Electronic Filing System employs the public key infrastructure to ensure the security of the Electronic Filing System proprietary network. Digital signature technology identifies persons who file documents using the system. The Key Management System caters for the issuance and management of smart cards and digital certificates. Every lawyer who is a registered user of the Electronic Filing System is issued with a smart card with its unique identity code and password – this is required before the lawyer can use the four services through the Web-based Front-End System.

Before a document can be filed electronically to the courts, it will have to be signed digitally. The digital signature is the key to the authenticity of the identity of the sender of the document and the key to the integrity and authenticity of the document. The smart card is required for penning the digital signature.

Commissioner for Oaths System

This system allows for the swearing or affirming of affidavits before Commissioners for Oaths electronically. It covers affidavits sworn/affirmed before both Judiciary and non-Judiciary Commissioners for Oaths.

3.10 STRATEGY BEHIND THE PLANNING, DEVELOPMENT AND IMPLEMENTATION OF THE ELECTRONIC FILING SYSTEM

From the inception of the planning and development of the Electronic Filing System, the Judiciary worked closely with the Law Society of Singapore, the Singapore Academy of Law and the Attorney-General's Chambers, together with the sole vendor of the project, CrimsonLogic (formerly known as Singapore Network Services Pte Ltd). It was of prime importance that all the major stakeholders in the legal fraternity were represented, as the success of the project was dependent on the acceptance by all the main players. Their input was invaluable because, ultimately, they would be the key users of the Electronic Litigation System.

On 8 March 1997, Phase 1.0 of the Electronic Filing System was launched. Phase 1.0 was implemented as a pilot programme to allow lawyers to experience the filing of documents electronically, and to identify the problems that arose from filing documents in this manner in order for these to be addressed and resolved. Electronic filing was on a purely voluntary basis. It covered limited types of documents in actions begun by a writ of summons. Selected law firms were provided with the necessary equipment and training to enable them to file documents electronically to the Supreme Court. The lessons learnt from three years of running Phase 1.0 were incorporated in the development of Phase 1.2.

There are five phases of implementation under the Electronic Filing System for civil matters. The target date for implementing the entire project is the end of 2002/2003. We decided to implement the Electronic Filing System in phases for a few reasons. One is to allow the legal profession to ease into a novel method of carrying out the business of litigation at a pace which will allow them to adequately adapt to working in an electronic environment. Secondly, the Electronic Filing System is a complicated system. Launching it over a few phases would mean that with each phase, we would have the benefit of improving on the system from the feedback of the users' experience in the previous phase. Thirdly, in terms of project management, it would be easier and more effective to manage the design and implementation of the Electronic Filing System in phases as the team can concentrate on smaller portions of this massive system and optimise its resources to ensure a timely launch of each phase. The schedule and scope of the five phases of the Electronic Fling System are:

Phase 1.2
Implementation Date: 1 March 2000
Scope: Writ of summons proceedings, including all applications and proceedings brought under or arising from such proceedings, but excluding interpleader proceedings, taxation of costs, District Court appeals and appeals to the Court of Appeal.

Phase 2
Implementation Date: 2 July 2001
Scope: Electronic Extract Service, Electronic Service of Documents Facility, Electronic Information Service, migration of the Front-End System from a Windows-based client server system on a private EDI network to a web application on the Internet.

Phase 3
Implementation Date: 18 December 2001
Scope: Originating summons, interpleader summons, proceedings, taxation of costs, District Court appeals, appeals to the Court of Appeal, admission of advocates and solicitors.

Phase 4(a)
Implementation Date: 3rd quarter 2002

Scope: Originating motions and petitions, admiralty, probate, bankruptcy, powers of attorney, petitions of course, companies' winding-up.

Phase 4(b)
Implementation Date: 4th quarter 2002
Scope: Divorce and family-related matters.

Phase 5
Implementation Date: 4th quarter 2002/1st quarter 2003
Scope: Migration of the antiquated Main Frame Civil System to the Electronic Filing System platform which will allow historical data of pre-Electronic Filing System matters to be stored in the Electronic Filing System.

With the launch of Phase 1.2 of the Electronic Filing System on 1 March 2000, there is compulsory electronic filing of court documents which fall within the Electronic Filing System regime to both the Supreme Court and the Subordinate Courts. Phase 1.2 covers most classes of court documents in writ actions. From our research, more than 80 per cent of the volume of documents filed to court is generated by writ of summons actions. Hence, a conscious effort was made to choose this class of actions as the first to be brought under the Electronic Filing System umbrella to ensure maximum impact and exposure to the Judiciary's e-revolution for the legal profession. The courts' business workflow in respect of the management of cases has been changed dramatically – an electronic workflow has superseded the paper workflow, from the processing of court documents to the fixing of hearing dates to the actual conduct of the hearings. It should be stressed that all hearings and trials within the scope of the Electronic Filing System have gone paperless. By the time Phase 1.2 was implemented, many lawyers had begun to adapt to hearings in an electronic environment.[12] Presently, the judges and registrars do not use paper case files, save for bundles of authorities, which can be submitted in paper at the hearing itself. All the courtrooms and chambers in the Su-

---

[12] This was as a result of the launch of the technology courts and the pilot implementation of the use of electronic documents in the courtroom.

preme Court have been refurbished and equipped to handle such hearings.

Phase 2 was launched on 2 July 2001. With this phase, the remaining three services of the Electronic Filing System, the electronic extracts service, the electronic service of documents facility and the electronic information service, are fully operational. Phase 2 also marks the migration of the Windows-based front-end system to the web. This has made the use of the services under the Electronic Filing System even more convenient for the lawyers. Phase 3 was launched on 18 December 2001. More classes of actions were brought under the Electronic Filing System umbrella, including originating summonses, taxation of costs, appeals to the Court of Appeal, the admission of advocates and solicitors, amongst others. Phases 4(a) and 4(b) will see the remaining classes of actions in civil litigation converted to the Electronic Filing System regime. Phase 5, which will be launched by early 2003, is a 'clean-up' phase. The antiquated Main Frame Civil System will be migrated to the Electronic Filing System platform. This will allow historical data of pre-Electronic Filing System cases to be stored in the Electronic Filing System database. There will no longer be two databases, one for paper cases and one for electronic cases. There will be one consolidated database which contains practically all the information on all civil cases in the Supreme Court and Subordinate Courts.

3.11   A WATERSHED IN THE PURSUIT OF AN ELECTRONIC LITIGATION SYSTEM

The implementation of the Electronic Filing System has proved to be a watershed in the Judiciary's pursuit of an Electronic Litigation System. Problems associated with the handling of paper are no longer a burden to the Judiciary. These problems include, *inter alia*, the non-filing and misfiling of documents, a long turn-around time in retrieving required documents and an ever-growing need for more physical storage space. The Electronic Filing System allows all documents to be stored in its database and the most up-to-date information on a case can be viewed by more than one person at the same time with the click of a button.

Law firms, too, benefit. They will no longer need to incur the time and money spent in making trips to the courts for the filing or the extraction of documents. The submission or extraction of court documents will be faster. In addition, the electronic filing service and the electronic service of documents facility will be available 24 hours a day, seven days a week. Law firms can thus submit their documents and serve documents on other law firms at their own convenience.

In a nutshell, the many benefits of the EFS include:

- improving efficiency by minimising paper flow to shorten case processing time;
- enabling the courts to be proactive in tracking the life span of cases;
- allowing concurrent access by different parties to view the same case file;
- facilitating faster document filing and retrieval;
- providing an integrated information service;
- a filing service which is available round the clock;
- minimising loss of documents due to misfiling or non-filing;
- providing a faster response as well as accurate and up-to-date information on cases.

There will also be no handling of cash since the Electronic Filing System is designed to enable electronic collection of fees. All these benefits translate into immediate savings in time and long-term savings in costs both for the Judiciary and the legal profession, and ultimately, the litigants.

Recently, there have been plans to extend the Electronic Filing System to all criminal matters in the Supreme Court. The development of Phase 6, which will cover High Court criminal trials, criminal appeals and magistrates' appeals, is still at an exploratory stage.

3.12 LawNet – a strategic national legal information network

LawNet is a strategic national information network within the legal sector that forms part of the information technology infrastructure of Singapore.

LawNet builds upon the various computerisation projects that the government has embarked upon in respect of the legal sector. It co-ordinates and
integrates all these efforts to create a national legal information database.
It enables a higher degree of standardisation and creates a more user-
friendly environment. The LawNet Council comprises the Honourable
Chief Justice as Chairman, the Minister of Law, the Honourable Attorney-General, the President of the Law Society of Singapore and the Dean
of the Faculty of Law at the National University of Singapore as members. LawNet operates as a one-stop centre for various information
repositories. Instead of having to arrange to gain separate access to the
databases of the Supreme Court, Registry of Companies, case law precedents, parliamentary debates and so on, lawyers and members of the public can get access to all these databases, and more, through LawNet.

LawNet was launched on 7 July 1990 with the implementation of an
electronic database of the statutes of Singapore. At present, the modules
under LawNet cover the major areas of legal practice, including:

- legal research (Legal Workbench);
- litigation;
- corporate law;
- conveyancing.

These modules allow the user to make searches for information relating
to Singapore registered companies and businesses, land title registration,
court cases such as bankruptcy and probate and electronic legal materials.

The Supreme Court is a key content provider to the litigation module
in LawNet, including case information on:

- writs of summons;
- admiralty;
- bankruptcy;
- companies' winding-up;
- taxation of costs;
- damages for personal injuries and death cases.

With LawNet, carrying out legal research becomes more convenient,
time-saving and more effective. Gone are the days when lawyers have to

spend hours in the library laboriously searching for precedents and authorities.[13]

3.13 THE FINAL PIECES OF THE ELECTRONIC LITIGATION SYSTEM JIGSAW – OTHER KEY APPLICATION SYSTEMS AND TECHNOLOGICAL INITIATIVES IN THE SUPREME COURT

To be a truly first-rate Judiciary, the courts should provide facilities which make it more convenient for lawyers and members of the public to use court services. In a similar vein, the training and welfare of the court staff should be looked after, and office facilities improved so that the work environment will be a conducive one. Over the years, the Supreme Court has implemented many other technological initiatives in our journey towards attaining world-class excellence in the administration of justice.

3.13.1 Practising Certificate E-filing System

Every year, during the peak period when lawyers file their applications for practising certificates in March and April, a lot of time and effort is taken up by staff in law firms, the Law Society of Singapore and the Supreme Court to fill in and process the applications before the practising certificate is issued by the Registrar of the Supreme Court. Very often, the Law Society and the Registry reject them for typographical errors and other minor inconsistencies and inaccuracies. Much time is spent shuffling paper from one person to another. These are all labour-intensive but menial tasks.

---

[13] The author will always remember those days in the distant past as a law student when she had to climb on to the shaky stools to reach for the dusty old All England Law Reports on the top shelf in the library, some copies of which were falling apart. It was truly a hazard to physical safety, as you never knew when your hand would slip and the whole shelf of books would come crashing down on your head. Now, it can be done in a matter of minutes with a computerised search using the LawNet system.

With the advent of the Practising Certificate E-filing System[14] on 1 March 2000, the business and administrative workings of the Supreme Court, the Law Society and the legal profession have been improved as applications for practising certificates have become an efficient and convenient process. The system allows lawyers to apply for the yearly renewal of their practising certificates on-line, cutting down on much paper work. Renewals of practising certificates can literally be obtained in seconds, with a soft copy of the certificate e-mailed to the lawyer.

3.13.2   Court information services

The Supreme Court Mobile Information Service, introduced in August 2001, enables any mobile phone user to request information on trials and hearings before judges and registrars virtually instantly. For instance, information on the name of the judge, the time and venue of the hearing will be sent by way of a short message to the requestor at no cost payable to the Supreme Court. The Supreme Court web site houses a wealth of information useful to both the public and legal researchers, including a history of the Judiciary, hearing lists, policies, procedures and practice directions, and Sheriff's sale of vessels. In the Supreme Court premises, there are interactive information kiosks or 'Infokiosks' which provide tourists and members of the public visiting the courts with useful information on the courts and serves as a guide around the courts.

3.13.3   Remote and wireless access to the Supreme Court network

The Supreme Court Local Area Network (LAN) is used daily by the Judges and Judicial Commissioners of the Supreme Court for on-line legal research, data retrieval and e-mail, among other applications. The conduct of court hearings in an electronic environment has increased the use of the network. Since July 2001, Judges and Judicial Commissioners are each provided with a laptop and have secured remote access to the Supreme Court network from their homes via the Citrix server. With this, they are able to work from the comfort of their home, carrying out legal

---

[14] The Practising Certificate E-filing System is accessible from the Supreme Court web site at <http://www.supcourt.gov.sg>.

research for the grounds of their decisions and reading electronic case files in preparation for their hearings. Remote access is being extended to registrars of the Supreme Court.

Wireless LAN infrastructure has also been installed in several 'hotspots' in the Supreme Court, for instance, in conference rooms, so that officers can have access to various applications on the LAN at meetings or discussions.

3.13.4 Internet Protocol videophone

On 19 February 2002, the Supreme Court introduced the use of the Internet Protocol (IP) videophone on a pilot basis for pre-trial conferences, matters heard before the Duty Registrar, ex-parte applications and other non-contentious applications heard by the registrars. This initiative allows lawyers, for the first time, to have their applications heard by the court without personally coming to court. Lawyers can simply call the registrar on the videophone, which is connected to a broadband IP network. The image of the caller is captured by a camera mounted on the phone set and transmitted to a small screen on the receiver's phone. With the videophone, the identity of the caller can be verified. The pilot run provides the legal profession with an effective visual communication conduit. This allows for enhanced productivity and communication between the law firm and the courts. Ultimately, this translates into savings to clients in legal fees.

3.13.5 Knowledge management and information repositories

Over the years, the Supreme Court has built up a valuable archive of information repositories. In addition to the Civil System, there are many other internal databases which form the nerve centre of our knowledge management, such as the Judgement Information Management System, repositories on press clippings and articles, internal policy directives and papers, case precedents, numerous other statistical and research data and a library enquiry system. These are utilised not only for legal research by the judges and judicial officers, but just as importantly, for the generation of reports, statistics and analyses, and the strategic planning process undertaken by senior management.

The Supreme Court has recently embarked on the Supreme Court Knowledge Management (KM) 21 project in February 2002. It seeks to consolidate the reforms and knowledge repositories of the past twelve years and to ensure continued excellence in judicial administration through advanced knowledge management tools, which will sit on Intranet technology. These tools will capture the tacit and institutional memory of the key decisions, problems and processes undertaken during the reform of the 1990s. These will assist the management and staff to engage in effective decision-making, notwithstanding changes in key personnel, by providing a rich historical base from which to evaluate future problems and to arrive at sound decisions. A detailed knowledge taxonomy of key data and statistics will also be created. Of equal importance will be a 'one-touch' knowledge management tool to allow for easy dissemination of all judicial decisions.

A related 'knowledge' initiative is the introduction of e-learning for the staff. In April 2002, an e-learning orientation package for new staff and those who require courses on all key aspects of court operations will have been made available. This will allow staff to become acquainted with court operations at their own time and pace. The scope of e-learning will be expanded in the training and development of the staff.

3.14   THE REALISATION OF THE VISION OF AN ELECTRONIC LITIGATION SYSTEM – THE DAWN OF A NEW ERA OF THE CYBERCOURT

The Singapore Supreme Court has come a long way in the use of court technology since its infant days at the beginning of the 1990s with the inception of the Main Frame Civil System. It is submitted that we have truly realised our vision of a total and integrated Electronic Litigation System. The Judiciary is moving towards the age of cybercourts. With the Electronic Filing System, the extensive video conferencing facilities and other telecommunication tools, the virtual courtroom is now a reality.

The Supreme Court's journey in the use of technology will culminate in the design and construction of the New Supreme Court Complex, which is planned to be completed in 2005. The futuristic and yet regal design of the New Building will be a fitting testimony of the successful reorganisation of the Judiciary in the past decade, in which the use of technology has played a key role. Come 2005, we will be working in a virtually electronic court environment in which all trials, court processes and transactions will be carried out electronically. State of the art technology will be a prime feature in the New Building, depicting a vibrant Judiciary well adept to meet the evolving needs of the community.

Wireless technology will be exploited. There are plans for extensive wireless facilities throughout the courthouse, tapping on the wireless LAN and wireless broadband infrastructure. We will have a multi-media digital recording facility to record proceedings in the court. A three-tier audio, visual and textual record of proceedings will be produced. Real time transcription of notes of evidence of court proceedings will be supported. The Supreme Court Intranet system will heighten the user-friendliness and utility of all the knowledge management tools and applications available. The whole building will be supported by a high bandwidth network that will facilitate high-speed links for broadband and video-streaming applications. There will be extensive use of video conferencing facilities, including video conferencing from the desktop, and a mobile commerce infrastructure to support mobile information services and transactions. There will be a centralised computerised resource management system which will manage the allocation and booking of court-rooms, chambers, meeting rooms and other court resources. An Infocommunications Resource Centre will be set up. Electronic signages, fully interactive information kiosks and a digital video wall-display in public areas will provide easy access to information on all aspects of the Supreme Court. The New Building will be an intelligent one in all its senses.

3.15 THE FINAL DESTINATION OF THE JOURNEY

It is hoped that this paper has provided a good overview of the use of technology in the Singapore Supreme Court to better the dispensation and administration of justice. We had failures, but we learnt from our mistakes. We initially faced strong resistance from the legal profession. Having to switch to working in a paperless environment is not easy, especially since we have all been brought up in a surrounding where paper is essential in our daily working and personal life. However, everyone has come to realise that these technological initiatives are big and definite steps which have to be taken in order for the Judiciary and the legal community to keep abreast of this fast-changing world which is increasingly dependent on technology and where business processes are constantly being streamlined. The Singapore Supreme Court's journey is a fine case study of how technology has helped in bringing about effective, efficient and economic dispensation and administration of justice. In the now-famous reorganisation of the Singapore Judiciary in the 1990s,[15] technology has played an important part.

The author would like to conclude with a quote from John Adams, the second President of the United States, which has had a profound influence on how she, as a judicial officer, perceives her responsibility to the community which she serves:

> 'The dignity and stability of government in all its branches, the morals of the people, and every blessing of society depend upon an upright and skilful administration of justice'.

In the final analysis, we should never lose sight of the fact that technology is but a means towards fulfilling the duty of every Judiciary in this world – that is the duty to uphold the rule of law through an upright and skilful administration of justice.

---

[15] The reorganisation of the Singapore Judiciary in the 1990s has prompted some commentators to refer to this period as the 'golden years of the Singapore Judiciary'. See the speech delivered by the Honourable Chief Justice Yong Pung How at a dinner on Saturday, 2 March 2002 in honour of Mr L.P. Thean on the occasion of the latter's retirement from the Supreme Court Bench.

Chapter 4
VENEZUELA

Ricardo Jiménez[1]

4.1 INTRODUCTION

Venezuela is a country with 24 million inhabitants spread over approximately 950,000 square kilometers, and is well-known for its petroleum industry and beaches. It is also a country that has in the last decade invested in the development of IT for the Judiciary, supported by a World Bank programme. Since the beginning of the 1990s, more and more emphasis has been placed on the use of Information Technology (IT) within the Judiciary. Traditionally, the courts in Venezuela were supported with little or even no IT,[2] but now that has changed. The focus of investment in IT support for the Judiciary is on legal changes, more transparency, a more efficient organization, access to users and integrating systems.

First of all, the structure of the Judiciary will be discussed, followed by some descriptions of the IT support tools presently available for the Venezuelan Judiciary.

---

[1] Due to language problems this report differs from the other reports in length and the amount of detail. It has been edited by the editors of this book. To enhance readability the structure has been adjusted and compressed, in order to avoid single line paragraphs.

[2] Waleed Haider Malik, 'Judicial Reform in Latin America: Towards a Strategic Use of ICT', in: Marco Fabri and Francesco Contini (Eds.), *Justice and Technology in Europe: How ICT is Changing the Judicial Business*, The Hague, Kluwer Law International, 2001, pp. 309-310.

A. Oskamp, et al. (Eds), IT Support of the Judiciary
© *2004, ITeR, The Hague, and the authors*

4.2   THE JUDICIARY

The legal system of Venezuela is based on legislation, not (only) on case law.

There is a difference between civil procedure, which is document-orientated, and criminal procedure, which is basically an oral procedure.

In 1999 a political reform process started in Venezuela. A new political constitution has since then changed the legal system and a new organization of justice was established. Before 1999 the Supreme Court was the highest instance in the legal system. Presently five powers can be classified within the Public Power Organization; executive, legislative, judicial, electoral and citizens' power. The judicial power is headed by the Supreme Tribunal of Justice (TSJ). The TSJ consists of six chambers for constitutional, civil, social, electoral, criminal and political matters.

The civil justice part of the TSJ employs about 650 judges in total. To be precise, at the moment of writing this report 646: 84 Higher Judges, 131 Judges of First Instance and 431 County Judges. Civil justice covers a broad range of topics: civil, commercial, administrative, labour, family, transit and agrarian topics.

The criminal justice part of the TSJ consists of 83 Courts of Appeal and 273 judges of First Instance.

4.3   INFORMATION AND COMMUNICATION TECHNOLOGIES IN THE JUDICIARY

Venezuela only recently started to explore the possibilities of technology for the Judiciary, first starting in the mid-1990s. The period 1996-2000 was used to identify strategical elements for justice. This identification was sponsored by the World Bank. In 2000 the strategic elements were even more emphasised after the government had declared the Internet to be a national priority for the development and economic growth of Venezuela.

The Venezuelan courts now have (in 2002) a high-level of hardware and software use. To illustrate this; the TSJ operates and uses ten servers using Windows NT as the operating system, over a thousand workstations with modern and fast Pentium III processors and around 100 printers. Other courts also make use of many servers and workstations. The systems within the TSJ are connected to each other and to the Internet. A national justice network is being developed and is expected to be finished by the end of 2002.

In Venezuela prosecutors and judges operate in isolation from each other. This also implies that they use different IT support tools. The only information we have available is on CMS for judges. Examples are the Case Management System (CMS) for judges which is different from the CMSs used by the public prosecutors. Judges use, for instance, a CMS called JURIS 2000. This system has both a criminal and a civil version for courts of appeal, superior judges, judges of first instance and county judges. JURIS 2000 was implemented in the second half of 1999 and has, amongst other things, the following functions (cf., Malik 2001):

- supporting the production of interactive documents;
- automatically integrating information stored in databases;
- adding new information to the database;
- automatically capturing information to avoid entering the same data;
- compiling information by using various sources;
- generating case delay warnings;
- generating information on case loads;
- sending information between judicial organisations;
- producing other (statistical) reports.

Another CMS used by the judges is the TEPUY XXI system, which is an integrated case management system for the Supreme Tribunal and which is linked to JURIS 2000. This system has many functions like a general record of description and events, an electronic diary, the timeliness of case progression and alerts, and the scheduling of cases. Figure 1 provides an impression of what this system looks like.

The TSJ uses production systems, case management systems, electronic filing systems, time standards and schedule systems. These systems have been developed by external software companies. There is also an Internet Portal (<www.tsj.gov.ve>) with information on justice, publications of all cases in full text and a jurisprudential database (see figure 2). This portal has been developed by the ICT department of the TSJ. Points of attention concerning the Justice's Portal are information and

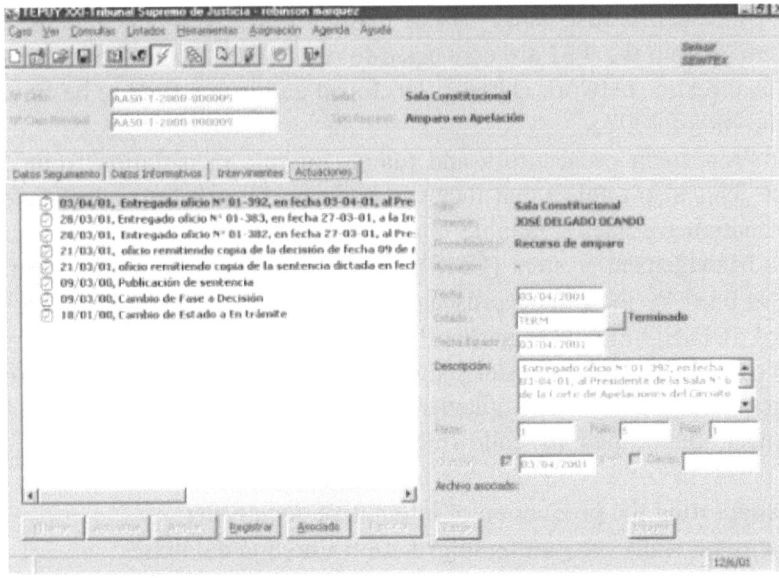

Figure 1. Example of a Case Management System

Figure 2. The Internet Justice Portal

contents administration, custom relationship management, organizational integration, business intelligence and knowledge management.

4.4   INTRODUCING IT

The initiation of IT projects for the Judiciary in Venezuela is not limited to a single organization. They can be initiated by the National Project for the Modernisation of Justice, by general policies, by judges and other, private, organizations proposing IT solutions to, for instance, the TSJ.

The drawbacks in introducing IT in Venezuela are first of all the costs which are inherent in IT and which are prohibitive for countries with poverty problems like Venezuela. Secondly, there is a resistance to change among the Judiciary.

Another point of attention is that IT influences legislation. This becomes clear when we see that the criminal code in Venezuela is being reformed by the National Assembly, a data messages and electronic signature law has been developed in 2001 and the TSJ will reach a decision as to how e-mail should be legally interpreted.

4.5   TRENDS IN IT

Besides worldwide popular concepts such as e-commerce and e-government we now also see e-justice. E-justice is becoming an important issue in Venezuela. Service to customers is one of the main issues. For this reason it has been made possible for the public to request information on cases and to be notified of progress in certain cases. This is partly supported by IT, for example the Case Management System can be accessed via the Internet. So, each participant in a case can retrieve relevant case information from the comfort of his/her own home. One can also subscribe to an SMS service, by which progress in a case is communicated directly to the subscriber.

The trends in IT in Venezuela mostly concern the Internet. Examples are the development of new web interfaces, the use of eXtensible Markup Language (XML), Java and wireless application formats such as WAP, SMS and Bluetooth (see, for example, figure 3). Another trend is also the use of open systems, using Linux as the operating system.

Figure 3. Wireless legal information

4.6   LEGAL INFORMATION KNOWLEDGE MANAGEMENT

Attention is devoted to Knowledge Management in the form of legal information knowledge systems, knowledge management systems, knowledge departments and the use of statistical information. Legal information is shared in various ways. Examples are sharing via the Internet (<www.tsj.gov.ve>), resources for training justice operators, academic forums and the Judiciary school (also e-learning). But also centres of teleservices belonging to Justice and virtual court buildings are being developed in order to share legal information. One of the aims of the legal information provision is to provide more legal information to more people and to bring people closer to IT and justice. Therefore we can also see the use of onsite centres such as the Centre for Document Information and the Citizen Orientation Office. Furthermore, for the purpose of knowledge management, extracts of jurisprudential databases have been created and expert networks have been developed and maintained.

Statistical information is used as part of business intelligence, decision support systems and data warehouses (in the future).

Chapter 5
IT IN THE NORWEGIAN COURTS

Morten S. Hagedal

5.1 INTRODUCTION

At the moment, the second wave of IT in the Norwegian courts is being developed and implemented. At the same time other major changes are taking place: the number of District Courts is being reduced from 92 to 65; with effect from 1 November 2002, a new National Court Administration has been set up; and the Land Registry is to be taken over by the National Mapping Authority.

The Norwegian Judiciary has used IT since the late 1980s. From the beginning a centralised approach has been chosen, hence all courts are provided with the same solutions. This made the Norwegian courts among the first to use IT on a broad scale, or to quote from the Norwegian report to the 10th Colloqium on Legal Data Processing in Europe in 1992:[1]

'There is hardly any country in the world where you will find a more uniform and widespread use of computers in the courts of justice than in Norway'.

All the courts have basically the same systems, based on minicomputers with 'intelligent' terminals. The number of terminals is roughly equivalent to the total number of judges and staff. As a consequence everyone who needs a terminal has one, and terminals also find their way into courtrooms.

After the implementation of the IT solutions around 1990 little occurred in this field for a number of years. Around 1995, the work on a new IT strategy for the Judiciary started, and new developments emerged

---

[1] Under the auspices of the Council of Europe (Cj-IJ), in Ankara, 5-7 October 1992.

A. Oskamp, et al. (Eds), IT Support of the Judiciary
© *2004, ITeR, The Hague, and the authors*

some years later. This IT strategy forms the basis for the current work being undertaken in the field of IT in the Norwegian Judiciary.

In this article, I will provide an overview of the development from the introduction of IT in the courts, as the Norwegian approach seems to differ from a number of other jurisdictions. It seems necessary, however, to provide a brief overview of the court structure, and the administration of the courts.

In the final part of the article, I will describe the current developments – or the second wave of IT in the Norwegian Judiciary.

5.2   The Norwegian Courts and the administration thereof

Norway has 96 courts; The Supreme Court, 6 Courts of Appeal, and 89 District Courts.

With a population of approximately 4.5 million covering an area of 324,220 square kilometers, with courts scattered around the country, some of them are necessarily rather small. Approximately 20 of the courts employ five persons: a registrar, a deputy judge and three administrative clerks. The larger courts are located in Oslo.

There are in total approximately 400 judges, and 150 deputy judges,[2] as well as 1000 administrative staff in the Norwegian Courts. Only the Supreme Court has law clerks, a total of 17.

In 2002, the District Courts decided the following number of cases:

Civil Cases	12,337
Summary Criminal Cases[3] and other criminal decisions	36,845
Ordinary Criminal Cases	16,845

---

[2] This is a rather peculiar feature of the Norwegian Judiciary; these positions are normally held by persons who have recently graduated from law school, and they have the same power as ordinary judges; to a large extent they act as ordinary judges. According to the Criminal Procedure Act, they may not hear criminal cases where the maximum sentence is more than six years imprisonment. A position as a deputy judge may be held for a maximum of three years.

[3] This is based on the Criminal Procedure Act s. 248, and is only used when the defendants provide testimony from which it is clear that the objective and subjective conditions for conviction are present. This should also be supported by other evidence, which is presented to the court in writing (i.e., police documents, witness statements, etc.).

During the same year the Courts of Appeal delivered judgements in the following number of cases:[4]

Civil Appeals	1809
Criminal Appeals (with a jury)	287
Criminal Appeals (without a jury)	947[5]

During the same year the Supreme Court delivered judgements in the following number of cases:

Civil Appeals	61
Criminal Appeals	87

The Interlocutory Appeals Committee in the Supreme Court delivered decisions in 772 civil and 819 criminal cases during the same year.[6]

One feature of the Norwegian court system is the Conciliation Boards. All civil cases are brought before these boards.[7] There is one Conciliation Board in each municipality, and each board consists of three lay members. It is within the power of the Boards to deliver decisions, including where the defendant does not reply to the writ of summons, hence the majority of cases are decided by these boards, and are not brought before the District Courts. The problems experienced in other jurisdictions concerning the amount of cases are therefore not present in the Norwegian Courts, as the administrative responsibility for these Boards is vested in the municipalities.

---

[4] The numbers for the Courts of Appeal and the Supreme Court are the cases actually decided by the said courts. A number of appeals is not admitted by the courts, as this is based on rulings by the Court of Appeal, or the Interlocutory Appeals Committee in the Supreme Court.

[5] In Hagedal (2001) the number of cases given for 1999 was 443; this, however, does not include criminal cases decided without lay judges. If the case on appeal only relates to sentencing, it is decided by judges alone, in other cases with lay judges. If the maximum sentence is more than six years imprisonment, there is a hearing with a jury.

[6] For more details see <http://www.domstol.no/Domstolene/index.asp?startID=&top Expand=1000010&subExpand=&menuitemid=1000337&strUrl=//internet/showObject. asp?i=1000415>.

[7] Cf., the Civil Procedure Act s. 272; there is a number of exceptions, cf., the Civil Procedure Act s. 273 and s. 274.

The general rule is that all courts have general jurisdiction within their geographical area.[8] All cases are brought before the District Courts, with the posssibility of appeal to the Court of Appeal. A further appeal might be brought before the Supreme Court, which might decide the case (i.e., it is not a *Cour de cassation*).

In addition to the ordinary tasks of the Judiciary, the courts are, for the time being, responsible for the Land Registry and some other administrative tasks. The Land Registry was important for the first wave of IT in the Norwegian Courts, see *supra*.

In 2001 it was decided that the responsibility for the Land Registry should be transferred from the District Courts to the Norwegian Mapping Authority, in order to facilitate a better co-ordination between the Land Registry and other services covering real estate.

The central court administration was vested in the Royal Ministry of Justice from its establishment in 1818 – four years after independence – until 31 October 2002. Effective from 1 November 2002 a semi-independent National Court Administration now has the responsibility for the administration of the courts. The Ministry of Justice does not have the power to instruct the National Court Administration. The guidelines for the National Court Administration are laid down annually by the executive and the legislative branch, and cover the goals for the Judiciary, but not the means by which to achieve these goals. For practical purposes this is done in conjunction with the annual budget. In exceptional circumstances the King (i.e., the cabinet) has the power to instruct the National Court Administration.

With the establishment of the National Court Administration, the former Norwegian State Court IT Service has turned into a part of the National Court Administration. This IT service was set up in 1995 to undertake the practical (but not necessarily strategical) tasks related to IT within the Judiciary. Prior to 1995 the practical handling of IT was undertaken by an enterprise, which from 1992 was owned by the state, represented by the Ministry of Justice.

---

[8] The only exceptions are the cities of Oslo, Bergen and Stavanger, where there is more than one court, and there has been a division of tasks among them. In cases concerning the unlawful dismissal of employees there is a limited number of courts which handle these cases.

Especially during in the 1990s each individual court has gained a stronger position concerning its internal administration, and power in a number of fields has been transferred from the Royal Ministry of Justice to each individual court. The larger courts employ administrative managers to assist the chief judges. There is reason to believe that this line will also be followed in the future, hence giving the individual courts a greater degree of self-governance.

5.3 CO-OPERATION AND CO-ORDINATION WITH THE OTHER LAW ENFORCEMENT AGENCIES – THE 'PENAL CHAIN'

Prior to the establishment of the National Court Administration the Ministry of Justice was responsible for the Police force and Prisons and Prohibition Officers, and had administrative responsibility for the Public Prosecutor, in addition to the courts. This made it possible to focus on the 'process' of dealing with offences and criminals.

At the same time, the political focus on co-operation and co-ordination has been strong, especially during the last decade. Due to a number of reasons few practical implications of this possibility have emerged over the years. It is easy to argue that the focus of the Ministry has not been on the practical implementation of co-ordinated solutions. At the same time, there was a struggle to cope with different priorities from the different agencies, and respectively within the different departments of the Ministry. Based on evaluations from the Auditor General, one might argue that the Ministry did not – to the necessary degree – actually co-ordinate its strategic approaches in the field of IT.

In its findings, the Office of the Auditor General states in the report to Parliament:[9]

'One finding of the study is that IT within the Criminal Justice Bodies is plagued by a lack of co-ordination, unclear signals from the Ministry of Justice, in combination with a lack of a strategic approach from the Ministry. With the lack of a co-ordinated approach there is a risk that the different agencies will give priority to their own inter-agency projects and measures'.

---

[9] Dok 3:5 (1998-1999) p. 1, my own translation.

Up until 1998 the Ministry did not have a common IT strategy for the handling of Criminal Cases. Based on the IT strategy a number of initiatives have been taken by the Ministry in order to obtain a better focus on this co-ordination and co-operation.[10] These initiatives will be mentioned briefly, in conjunction with actual developments within the Judiciary.

5.4   THE FIRST WAVE OF IT IN THE NORWEGIAN COURTS

The rationale for the introduction of IT in the Norwegian Courts in the late 1980s was the Land Registry. At that time the relevant information on each item of property was written on a sheet of paper (size A3), and stored in large boxes. This process was time consuming, and some of the courts had severe backlogs.

IT was to be be obtained for the Land Registry. A new approach was chosen; an agreement was entered into with a private enterprise, which was to develop the necessary software, and acquire the hardware and shelf-ware. This company, in return, would obtain a monopoly on the sale of land registry information.[11]

The agreement also covered the other IT solutions mentioned in this part.

With this approach, two goals were achieved. The general problem of funding, as the budget is decided annually, is probably the most obvious. At the same time, it would be difficult for the Ministry to undertake the practical responsibilities involved in implementing IT. This task had – to a certain degree – to be undertaken by a project organisation outside the Ministry.

Two existing companies owned the company Tinglysingsdata AS – literally translated as Land Registry Data. However, it transpired that the income from the sale of land registry information did not amount to the required revenue. In 1991[12] the Ministry of Justice obtained permission

---

[10] Cf., Skagemo and Høvik (2002) for a broader presentation of these initiatives.

[11] This agreement has been extended, with the latest agreement running from 1st January 2000 to 31st December 2004. According to the last agreement, the company is obliged to finance the new Land Registry Software to be used by the new Land Registry Authority, cf., *supra* 5.2.

[12] Cf., St.prp. No. 70 (1990-91) and St.prp. No. 1 (1991-92), appendix 3.

from Parliament to acquire the company. For the acquisition of the company, the state paid about 200 million NOK. It turned out that the necessary revenue for the company was obtained – only a few years later than predicted. After the establishment of the Norwegian State Courts' IT Service this company changed its name to Norsk Eiendomsinformasjon AS.

In the years 1988-1993 the following IT was implemented in the courts:

5.4.1 Technical infrastructure

The solution of UNIX machines within each court was chosen, and there was no WAN for the courts. However, an x.25 solution was chosen for the transfer of data from the local land registry bases to the central land registry base. The user was presented with an x-windows terminal, and WordPerfect as a standard package. In addition came the developed software. All software was developed with a character-based user interface.

With the UNIX solution it was possible to access the machines in each court from a central point, hence making trouble-shooting possible without travelling to each destination in the country, thereby establishing a rather cost-effective solution.

5.4.2 Land Registry

The Land Registry formed the 'backbone' of the solution. The task of converting the information from the above-mentioned sheet to a database was rather time- and cost-consuming. The company Tinglysingsdata AS undertook this task.

The system is based on one *local* data base in each court in which the data is registered, and one *central* database, to which the data is transferred during the evening. The latter is the *official land registry data base*, and is used for the dissemination of data. The reason for choosing this solution lies, simply, in the communication solutions of the late 1980s. Establishing one central data base, and on-line access thereto was considered too vulnerable.

5.4.3   Case management system

A case management system was developed for the courts.[13] The system is mainly used by office staff, and has to some degree relieved them of manual tasks. Typically, the system is used for registration purposes in each case – the writ of summons and subsequent writs are recorded in the system. The system is used for all cases handled by the courts, with the exception of land registration, marriage and other notary public tasks, and some tasks regarding guardians.

The relevant information is also used for management information, see *supra*.

Each court has its own system, and there is no transfer of data between the different courts. All District Courts and all Courts of Appeal use the same system.

The Supreme Court does not use this CMS, and has never done so. It is rather unclear why they have chosen not to do so. While all the other courts were *instructed* to use the CMS, the Ministry chose not to compel the Supreme Court to do so. The reasoning of the Supreme Court is not easy to discern, but it seems that the argumentation presented was that the CMS did not fit the needs of the Supreme Court.

5.4.4   Accounting software

Standard accounting software was also implemented in the courts. It might seem surprising today, but there is no transfer of data between the case management system, the land registration system, and the accounting system, hence certain data are registered twice, or even more than this in each court.

5.5   SOME EFFECTS OF THE INTRODUCTION OF IT, AND SOME OTHER AIMS OF THE COURT ADMINISTRATION

The CMS may be used for statistical purposes, which is largely being done. Since each court has its own database, it is not possible to collect

---

[13] It might be argued that this system does not qualify as a case *management* system, but the term has nevertheless been ascribed to this system.

data from all the courts as an on-line search. However, some data have been collected periodically by the Ministry of Justice, and some of this has been compiled. Most probably, the National Court Administration will continue doing the same.

Before moving on to the possibilities for obtaining statistics, I will mention two aspects that are fundamental for the statistics obtained by the Ministry.

5.5.1 Time standards

Norway is one of the few jurisdictions where the court administration has developed time standards for the courts. These were developed in 1990-1991, and they have been retained by the Ministry ever since.[14]

Each court is supposed to have an average time for dealing with cases, and is to report if the time standards are not being met. The time standards for the District Courts are:

A (Ordinary Civil Cases)	6	months
F (Summary Criminal Cases)[15]	1	month
M (Ordinary Criminal Cases)	3	months
Land Registration	1-2	days

5.5.2 The reduction of employees – the required staff in a specific court

The introduction of IT boosted the effectiveness of the courts, especially with regard to land registration. Due to this, it was necessary to reduce the number of employees in the courts. It was estimated that a 30 per cent reduction in the clerical staff would be reasonable. It turned out that this was a rather accurate estimate.

---

[14] The time standards have been presented to Parliament, which seems to have approved them. It is unclear, however, whether the time standards are supposed to form part of the guidelines set for the National Court Administration and the Judiciary; the reason for this is simply unfortunate editing and presentation by the Ministry of Justice. Most likely, this will be solved by the annual budget for 2004.

[15] See n. 3.

At that time, the Ministry had not developed any objective criteria for the number of judges and employees in each court. There was a need for an objective instrument in this respect.

A model for staffing was developed. Judges and clerical staff had to record the time which they expended in fulfilling their tasks over a period of two months, and this was used as a basis for the model.

For each group of cases the average time expended by judges and administrative staff was calculated based on the said empirical data. In developing this model, there was no attempt at evaluating the actual time required, or trying to make the courts more efficient.

This model had two purposes: In reducing the number of employees in the courts, it was used as a starting point in defining the number of employees in each individual court. No employees were dismissed; the reduced numbers were based on persons voluntarily leaving their position, typically retiring, or finding a new post. Regarding the latter, around 20 persons were transferred to other criminal justice agencies.

In Norway, the general principle is that the calculated effectiveness should be highlighted in the relevant budgets, i.e., the court budgets. However, an understanding with the Ministry of Finance was obtained, after which most of the reduced funding was returned to the courts, opening the way for a more formalised education programme for judges and administrative staff, and a change in the administrative staff who had obtained higher paid positions.

After the reduction of employees the model – or rather the model used for each individual court – is used in deciding on an application from a court for an increase in judges or clerical staff. If the model indicates that the particular court is adequately staffed, there has to be a good reason as to why the model is not satisfactory for the individual court. At the same time, if the model indicates that the court is understaffed, there is a good possibility for obtaining funding for additional staff.

This model has some obvious weaknesses, in that there are no factors which indicate whether the case is important or minor, or how long the court will remain in session for each case. The model has also been criticised by the larger District Courts in the larger cities, arguing that the cases handled by those courts are more complex, hence more time-consuming, than the average indicated by that model. There are two different versions of the model, depending on the size of the court, and a third for courts that only handle ordinary civil and criminal cases. To a certain degree this does resolve the referred to criticism.

Now there is discussion on further developing the model, but there is no statistical information to support such a development. It seems that this is partly due to incorrect information regarding the hours in session in each case. This was addressed in 1998, and data from then and subsequently should be more accurate.

5.5.3   Statistics by the court administration

During the initial years after the implementation of the CMS, each court had to complete a form which was sent to the Ministry. This has now been altered, so the relevant data are extracted and automatically transferred to the Ministry, and the National Court Administration maintains the same system.

Time standards are essential. For each court the time expended in the different cases are complied, with parameters on average time usage, the number of cases filed with the court, the number of cases decided, and the backlog is also shown in these statistics.[16]

The average for each court is then complied, and this provides an accumulated statistic for the courts.

These statistics are published twice annually by the Ministry of Justice, in addition to being presented on the web. Probably the National Court Administration will uphold this tradition.

5.5.4   Statistical possibilities for each court

In each court there is a search facility in the CMS, making it possible for *each user* to generate relevant information on the number of cases filed, the number of cases decided, the average time expended, the backlog, the oldest undecided case, and the number of hours in session; for the court as such, for a particular department within the court,[17] or concerning an individual judge.

---

[16] A portion of these statistics is available at <http://www.domstol.no/Domstolene/index.asp?startID=&topExpand=1000010&subExpand=&menuitemid=1000337&strUrl=//internet/showObject.asp?i=1000415> in Norwegian.

[17] Only the major District Courts are divided into departments, in addition to two Courts of Appeal.

This might be used by the administrative managers in the court, but also by any curious judge or employee. It might be a relevant tool in deciding the allocation of new cases to judges.

It is unclear to what extent this is being used by the individual courts, and for what purpose, as this possibility has never been evaluated by the Ministry. The impression, however, is that some courts have been keen on using statistics, while others are more reluctant in this respect.

5.6 DISSEMINATION OF CASES

Unlike some other jurisdictions the courts, or the government for that matter, has not had a central role in the dissemination of cases in Norway. Traditionally there are two Case Law Reports, published by the Norwegian Bar Association, one covering all judgements and some of the other decisions from the Supreme Court, the other covering the Courts of Appeal and the District Courts.[18]

The Lovdata foundation[19] was established in 1981, by means of an agreement between the Ministry of Justice and the Foundation publishing the compilation of statues.[20]

The aim of Lovdata was from the beginning to become *the* legal information system for Norway, a status which it has now acquired. Statutes and regulations are provided free of charge on the World Wide Web, together with recent decisions from the Supreme Courts and the Courts of Appeal.

From the beginning of 1987 the Supreme Court has sent all its decisions to Lovdata. The Lovdata foundation later entered into an agreement

---

[18] At the same time, it should be mentioned that the Government has not adopted any strong position with regard to the consolidation of legislation. The consolidation of legislation has been undertaken by a foundation which has strong ties with the Faculty of Law at the University of Oslo. This foundation is responsible for the biannual compilation of statutes in force. However, the Ministry of Justice also took part in establishing this foundation.

[19] <http://www.lovdata.no>.

[20] The agreement and the regulations for the Lovdata foundation are published in Selmer (1981).

with Eidsivating Court of Appeal[21] on 16th December 1991, according to which all judgements and some other decisions should be transferred to Lovdata, the judges write the summaries themselves, and the Court of Appeal has free access to the on-line services of Lovdata. Later on, the other courts of appeal entered into similar agreements; Hålogaland on 21st December 1992, Frostating on 30th December 1992, Agder on 6th January 1993, and Gulating in April 1993. Finally, an agreement was entered into with Eidsivating on 17th October 1995, some three months after that court was established.[22]

These agreements are entered into by the individual courts, and are not maintained by the Ministry of Justice, nor the National Court Administration.

5.6.1   Recourse: Lovdata

The Lovdata foundation has with its latest on-line client included a new feature for statistical sentencing information on alcohol-related driving offences and possession of narcotics. This search facility provides access to the summaries of the cases, and does not include any graphical presentation – like, for example, the system used by the High Court in Edinburgh.

5.7   SENTENCING SUPPORT

5.7.1   A Sentencing Support System for the Judiciary?

In one of the working groups for the IT strategy for the Judiciary (1997-2001), Judge Stein Schjølberg proposed the development of a Sentencing Support System. The background to this proposal is probably the work undertaken in this field in other jurisdictions, and the personal involve-

---

[21] The Court of Appeal located in Oslo was called Eidsivating. This court was divided into two courts from 1st August 1995, the larger one, located in Oslo, being called Borgarting, and the smaller one located in Hamar retained the name Eidsivating. Actually all courts of appeal are named after Viking Kings.

[22] All dates referred to were provided by the Lovdata foundation on 20th March 2000.

ment of Mr Schjølberg in this respect. In arguing why the strategy did not include such a proposal I am – primarily – resoring to guesswork.

Firstly, the development of a CMS for the courts would probably have higher priority. Faced with the limited general financial support for IT in the courts this argument seems plausable.

Secondly, unlike most jurisdictions there has not been any general discussion on sentencing discrepancies in Norway, neither in the public (political) discussion nor in legal circles. Neither has there been much discussion on whether the legislature should provide more guidelines for sentencing. The public discussions have rather been oriented towards the general level of sentencing: whether sentences should be increased or not.

Traditionally the legislature has provided maximum, and in some cases minimum, sentences for each offence, and the courts generally decide in each case based on relevant decisions from the Supreme Court, and from 1995 onwards, from the Courts of Appeal. Only with regard to alcohol-realted driving offences have there been some attempts to standardise sentencing by the legislature.

It is my impression that in some of the jurisdictions where Sentencing Support Systems have been developed there have indeed been such discussions, which to some degree has given credence to the development of Sentencing Support Systems.

Thirdly, with the former courts administration it is doubtful whether it would be within the traditional division of power to develop such a tool. Developing a system based on *norms* is difficult. One possibility would be that a independent entity could develop such a system, not approved by any public entity, but it is doubtful whether such a system would be accepted on a general basis.

A purely statistical system is an alternative. This has some disadvantages. As Norway has no strong *stare decisis* doctrine, the Supreme Court stated in a number of cases in the 1990s that in general sentences have to be increased for some fallonies. In some cases the Supreme Court has gone in the opposite direction, e.g., possession of heroin. Due to this there are some obvious limitations with a purely statistical system, which have to be overcome on a theoretical level.

5.7.2   A Sentencing system for Public Prosecutors?

Some of the difficulties regarding a sentencing system are pertinent to the courts. For the public prosecutors the situation is different.

It is within the powers of the head of the public prosecution service to issue guidelines to public prosecutors. This is sometimes done regarding sentencing. These guidelines are communicated to the public prosecutors in writing, and are normally only rough guidelines.

It seems to fall within the authority of the head of the prosecution service to develop a fully norm-based system for sentencing support, with some limitations. This has not been done, however, and it does not seem to be planned for the future.

5.8   THE SECOND WAVE OF IT IN THE NORWEGIAN JUDICIARY

5.8.1   The starting point for the second generation of IT in the Norwegian Judiciary

After the implementation of the IT solutions in the late 1980s and early 1990s there was little in the way of development for a number of years. The year 1995 seems to be the point when new initiatives appeared. The work on a new IT strategy for the Judiciary started, and the foundations were laid for further development.

It was clear that the existing systems had become outdated, and new initiatives were necessary. During the work with the new IT strategy new initiatives were formed, and these have also been followed in subsequent years. The strategy only became operational toward the end of 1997.[23]

The key elements in the strategy are:

- the development of a WAN;
- the development of a new CMS for the courts;
- the development of a new Land Registry System;

---

[23] The draft for the strategy was completed in the summer of 1996, but the general hearing and the following work in the Ministry unfortunately took 18 months. One could easily argue that this is not an acceptable situation.

- the development of a common portal for the Judiciary on the web;
- the development of an Intranet for the courts;
- the introduction of e-mail;
- the implementation of a new accounting system.

In parallel with the development of the strategy two new Case Management Systems were developed: a CMS for marriages and a CMS for the Supreme Court. I will mention these before going on to describe the developments following the IT strategy.

5.8.2   Case Management System for marriage

As indicated *supra* the District Courts judges are also notaries public, and in this respect, they are empowered to conduct a marriage ceremony. The courts are the only forum for entering into a marriage outside a religious context.[24]

In 1996 a CMS for marriages was developed. This is an application developed for a Win 3.11 operating system, and the first GUI ever developed for the Norwegian Courts. The system has the same functionality as the CMS for other cases, although the relevant information *has* to be entered.

5.8.3   Case Management System for the Supreme Court

Parallel with the development of the IT strategy, and the future CMS for the Norwegian Courts, a CMS has been developed for the Supreme Court. The Courts' IT service has been responsible for this application. The project was instigated, however, in close co-operation with the Supreme Court and the independent developer contracted for this CMS – Computas.[25] The CMS has been operational since December 1999.

As mentioned, in *supra* 5.4.3, the Supreme Court chose not to use the CMS developed in the late 1980s. The initiative for the CMS came from the Supreme Court.

---

[24] It should here be mentioned that two Chief Constables are also notaries public, and are hence also empowered to conduct marriage ceremonies.

[25] <http://www.computas.no/>.

The Supreme Court is not that different from the other courts regarding the general case flow. Due to this, there was an alternative to develop a separate module for the Supreme Court. One of the reasons for independently developing this CMS was that it was the first major development project in more than ten years, and for the Court IT service and the Ministry this was a welcome initiative before the larger development projects which were to follow in the near future.

The Supreme Court (normally) consists of 18 judges with a support staff of legal clerks and administrative staff. Five judges sit in session, two divisions at the same time. In extraordinary cases a case is decided by a plenary session. In addition, there is the Interlocutory Appeals Committee of the Supreme Court – a board of three judges which handles a number of cases with a written procedure. This includes applications for appeal to the Supreme Court, deciding procedural appeals, and appeals where there has been a decision – not a judgement – at the Court of Appeal.[26]

The major users of the CMS were thought to be the clerks and administrative staff. It was decided by the Supreme Court, at an early stage, that the judges should have the option of not using the system.

The case flow in the Supreme Court forms the basis of the system, which includes *mandatory* and *non-mandatory* tasks to be undertaken at each stage of the case. The mandatory tasks are those necessary for the following task, either based on the Criminal Procedure Act, or the Civil Procedure Act, or because the Supreme Court has decided that it is a mandatory task during the development of the CMS. The last-mentioned category is based on the internal procedures of the Court.

The feedback from the users has so far been rather positive. A number of proposed amendments have been put forward. It is our opinion that a majority of these are due to a lack of knowledge concerning the development process; partly because of computer illiteracy in the Supreme Court, and partly because the input from the Supreme Court has not been scrutinised from 'the other side'.

There is no communication between the CMS and other systems, with the exception of transferring decisions to Lovdata.

---

[26] The latter category is the result of the Criminal and Civil Procedure in the subordinate courts, and covers a number of different cases.

The CMS is used by the staff – as predicted. Somewhat surprising, however, is the widespread use by the judges. A majority of the judges use the CMS when sitting in the Interlocutory Appeals Committee. It appears that they have realised that the relevant information is more easily available from the CMS than from any other source.

5.8.4   Wide Area Network, thin clients and standard software

A new concept for general infrastructures has been decided and developed. The implementation in all Norwegian Courts was finalised in October 2003. The new concept is based on a common Wide Area Network,[27] 'thin clients' based on Citrix and Windows 2000 in combination with the MS Office package.

At the same time, all users within the courts are provided with e-mail accounts and access to the web. With the use of thin clients, data protection might more easily be solved than with traditional PCs in the network.

At the same time, there is a project to introduce e-mail for the police, the public prosecutors and the prison and probation authorities. This makes possible the use of e-mail with attachments. The problems of privacy and data protection have been resolved by the use of dedicated lines between the three WANs, using encrypted lines.

5.8.5   Intranet

So far, no Intranet system has been developed for the Judiciary. This decision seems to have followed two lines. One is that each court has the possibility to establish its own Intranet, based on a software package obtained by the Norwegian State Court IT Service. Some larger courts have made use of this opportunity, and have developed their own Intranet.

After the establishment of the National Court Administration, it seems that the administration has a desire to establish one common Intranet for all the courts. The details in this respect are not clear.

5.8.6   Land Registration

As mentioned, *supra* 5.2, the task of land registration is to be removed from the courts to the Mapping Authority. As a result, the responsibility

---

[27] The network is based on IP VPN.

for the case management system will follow. In 2000 the Ministry of Justice entered into an agreement with Company Norsk Eiendomsinformasjon, cf., *supra* 5.4, on the development of a new CMS for land registration purposes. This system will allow the introduction of electronic documents. The new system will, probably, enter into production in 2004.

5.8.7 A portal for the Judiciary on the web

The establishment of a portal for the Judiciary on the web has taken place.[28] This portal has some general information on the courts, contact information for all the courts, information on the National Court Administration, as well as statistical information.

Any further development of the portal is largely up to the individual courts, as each court has the possibility to establish its presence within the frames of this portal. Each court also has the possibility to publish its calendar of cases for the general public, and also to set up specific pages for the media.

5.8.8 CMS for the District Courts and the Courts of Appeal – LOVISA

The development of a new Case Management System for the District Courts and the Courts of Appeal has been in operation since February 2001.[29] Due to the rather long period of development, the CMS will be delivered in two parts. The delivery of part 1 took place in February 2003, and is being implemented in the courts at this very moment. Part 2 will be delivered in April 2004. LOVISA is based on the same underlying principles as the CMS for the Supreme Court, cf., *supra* 5.8.3.

From the start, there was a strong focus on electronic communication between different courts, and between the courts and other parties. The aim was to introduce electronic communication to a large extent. However,

---

[28] Cf., <www.domstol.no>.

[29] Prior to this there was a 'pre-project' from 1998 to 1999 which assessed the possibilities for a new system, also laying the principles for development. The project is based on an iterative method, and not a full specification of the software.

the Ministry had difficulties with founding, and almost all electronic communication was removed from the agreement with the provider.

The system will use one central database for all the courts; hence, all data and documents will be available to the courts which require them.[30] There will also be integration with other applications used by the courts, in order to fulfil the requirement that information should be entered into one system, and be transferred to other systems.

There are developments in the direction of e-filing,[31] in the first part of LOVISA, and there is a rather basic solution for communication between the prosecutors of the lower tier[32] and the courts. This is based on XML Schema, and a SMTP-based transfer. This falls within the responsibility of the Ministry of Justice, cf., *supra* 5.3. One important point, however, is that the paper version of the case also has to be transferred, as security within this system is not sufficient. The reason for choosing such a solution has been the available time for development and the political desire to have a working system by the summer of 2003, in combination with the development of LOVISA.

Within the current development, the National Court Administration is working to establish a general method for – primarily – asynchronous communication. One solution that will be in place with the second delivery of LOVISA is the transfer of information from the National Companies Register to the courts and information from the courts to the Bankruptcy Register. This will also be based on XML Schemas, but the communication will be with a standard software package for communication,[33] resulting in a better method for controlling the actual communication. With this solution all transfers of paper documents – in this field – will vanish. Hopefully, this solution has the necessary potential for development with other parties, and synchonus communication, that

---

[30] However, there are some measures in the system designed to block unauthorised access, so it would be more accurate to stress that information is made available in certain circumstances. However, the information should be made available when necessary.

[31] System-to-system communication between the courts and parties.

[32] The prosecution authority is divided into three levels: there is one Advocate General, and his cabinet, there are regional prosecutors, and there are prosecutors within the police force.

[33] MS BizTalk.

hopefully will be developed – at last with the entry into force of the new Civil Procedure Act, *supra*.

The actual project consists of approximately 55 persons,[34] most of whom work less than 50 per cent on the project. In addition to the project management, there are judges, clerical staff, technicians and organisational experts within the project organisation. The introduction of such a complex system requires a strong focus on organisational development.

5.8.9 Further developments

On the basis of what has been described, a good foundation has been formed for further integration projects. There is a new ICT strategy for the courts (2002-2005) that gives some indications as to what is necessary during that period. Most of these aims are covered by existing projects.

At the same time, the necessary legislative amendments are in place in order to allow electronic communication with the courts. In the short term, this has been solved with an amendment to the Courts Act which simply states that electronic communication with the courts is permitted; even if existing provisions are contrary to this. In the longer term, there is a proposal for a new Civil Procedure Act, that has some regulations which are of interest, *inter alia*, that attorneys are required to communicate electronically with the courts.

The LOVISA project has set up a general framework for electronic communication. As far as the project and the National Court Administration are concerned, the desired standard for format is XML. The courts should be able to communicate over a number of different infrastructures, based on the possibilities of the parties with whom the courts actually communicate.

How this general framework will actually be used remains to be seen, but the impression is that a number of parties will be interested in such electronic communication, including the Norwegian Bar Association.

I presume that further developments in electronic communication, to a large extent based on e-filing, will be the major step forward in the com-

---

[34] July 2003.

ing years. At the same time, amendments to LOVISA must be made, in order to support the new Civil Procedure Act.

5.9 BIBLIOGRAPHICAL REFERENCES

DOK 3:5 (1998-1999) Riksrevisjonens undersøkelse vedrørende styring og samordning av IT-virksomheten i Justissektoren

HAGEDAL (2001), Morten S., 'Norway: practical perspective', in: Lodder et al., *IT Support of the Judiciary in Europe*, ITeR No. 43, The Hague, Sdu 2001

SELMER (1981), Knut (ed.) The Lawdata Papers; *CompLex 7/81*, Oslo

SKAGEMO AND HØVIK (2002); Steinar Skagemo and Kathrine Høvik, *Judicial Electronic Interchange in European Civil Proceedings and Criminal Matters – Norway*, Forvaltningsinformatisk notatserie 2/02, available from <http://www.afin.uio.no/forskning/notater/index.html>

Chapter 6
THE NETHERLANDS

Arno R. Lodder, Anja Oskamp and Ronald van den Hoogen

6.1 INTRODUCTION

After tentative plans in the 1970s, the actual use of computers in criminal proceedings really started in the 1980s. At the beginning of this century, viz., 2003, most parts of the judicial organization are automated, or, to put it differently, are supported by Information Technology (IT). As far as civil and administrative procedures are concerned a similar development can be recognized.

6.2 IT SUPPORT FOR JUDGES CONCERNING SENTENCING DECISIONS

Both the acknowledgment of the inconsistency problem and the need for judicial sentencing that does not depend too much on prosecution policy, have resulted in the developed of a statistical system for the Judiciary (NOSTRA), inspired by the Scottish Sentencing Information System (Hutton et al., 1996). It delivers statistical figures relating to sentences passed in previous cases that are considered to be alike on the basis of limited concepts.[1] Because the number of concepts is rather small, sometimes a retrieved case is not relevant because of other concepts that have not been taken into account. Therefore, the information which judges obtain from the system needs to be seen in perspective. The technical evalu-

---

[1] Typologies of offences are used. This means that the offences in the system are not necessarily the offences that are formulated in the Criminal Code. Instead, offences are formulated as factual complexes that often come before the court (e.g., handbag 'snatching').

A. Oskamp, et al. (Eds), IT Support of the Judiciary
© *2004, ITeR, The Hague, and the authors*

ation of the system has not been very positive.[2] The technical as well as the organizational management of information needs to be improved.

The lack of information concerning the reasons why colleagues decide to impose a specific sentence is considered to be a possible cause of the inconsistency in judicial sentencing. In order to provide judges with better information about sentencing (considerations) in like cases, the Ministry of Justice supported a project that resulted in an advanced retrieval system for similar cases: IVS (E.W. Oskamp 1998).[3] The system uses many concepts to determine whether cases are similar. IVS very efficiently retrieves and presents the arguments and considerations used for the sentences which are imposed in similar cases.

At the end of 1999 the CST (Consistent Sentencing) project started, whose objective was to develop a database that will be easier to use and maintain than IVS. Two years later, this database was presented. The characteristics used by E.W. Oskamp were reduced to a minimum, but included basically the criteria type of offence, first offender, and the age of the offender. The database can currently be used by judges via Intranet, but in the coming years the Judiciary wants to make the database available to attorneys as well as the general public.

6.3   IT SUPPORT FOR THE PROSECUTOR CONCERNING SENTENCING REQUESTS

In 1989 an Act was introduced, known as 'de Wet Mulder' (The Mulder Act), that deals with the automated handling of certain traffic violations. For example, in cases of driving through a red light or exceeding the speed limit, almost without human intervention this violation automatically results in a pre-printed giro credit slip that is sent to the violator.

A more recent initiative is the support of the public prosecution service by a decision support system. In general, the prevention of inconsistent

---

[2] This also has to do with the fact that the necessary organization for filling the system with cases lacks efficiency.

[3] The realized implementation is the starting point for a currently running project coordinated by the five appeal courts. The implementation needs to be evaluated for that purpose.

sentencing leads to measures to attach fixed penalties to specific offence descriptions. Naturally, IT is an important tool to support this objective of consistency. The public prosecution service has introduced prosecuting guidelines and their application is supported by the rule-based (decision tree) decision support system BOS (POLARIS 1997). This system provides advice to the prosecutor as to which sentence should be demanded.[4] The prosecutor needs to answer certain questions about the facts and circumstances of the case, e.g., 'the amount of money stolen', 'the use of a weapon' or 'the violence used towards the victim'. The system translates those answers (e.g., 'more than € 1000', 'yes', 'little') into points and percentages. At the end the system converts the points and percentages into a particular sentence to be demanded, from which the prosecutor can only deviate if he has sound reasons therefor.[5]

As of December 2002 the BOS programme can be downloaded via <www.om.nl/bos>.

6.4   IT SUPPORT FOR JUDGES IN DETERMINING DAMAGES

A programme called DOLOR has been on the market since the late 1980s. It can be used by judges for determining damages, in particular concerning personal injuries. DOLOR is a commercial programme, published by the ANWB (the Dutch Road Users' Association). This programme provides details on amounts of damages awarded by the courts and published in the journal *Road Traffic Law* (in Dutch: *Verkeersrecht*). It contains abstracts from case law on damages. It is possible to search the cases using various described criteria. This year a new and modern version of the DOLOR programme will be published by the Dutch publisher Kluwer. There is no information available as to whether this programme is presently being used by judges.

---

[4] The advice does not necessarily have to be a specific sentence which should be demanded before court. Generally, BOS advises as to how to settle a case. This advice could also be, for example, an out-of-court settlement.

[5] Through a method of the decreasing penal value of offences, the system takes into account the fact that the accumulation of offences can result in extremely severe sentences being demanded.

6.5 MANAGEMENT INFORMATION TO EVALUATE THE PRODUCTIVITY AND/OR QUALITY OF JUDGES

In the mid-1990s a programme called RAPSODY was introduced to generate management information. It derives information from the administrative systems that are used by the Judiciary (see *infra* 6.12): COMPAS (criminal proceedings), BERBER (administrative proceedings), and 'Civiel Rechtbank' (civil proceedings). Besides periodical overviews of a number of cases that have come before the courts and their outcome, it is also possible to formulate an individual query. In the latter case information is generated upon demand. In criminal proceedings a system called CEBRA is used to output on demand. A special server is used to answer the SQL-like queries that can be sent by e-mail using the CEBRA system.

Judges generally do not like their performance to be evaluated by quantitative means such as management information. Judges fear that the use of management information could force them to work faster and thereby less accurately. This is not an unrealistic fear, because of the fact that courts are nowadays funded according to the number of cases they handle.

6.6 ON MANAGEMENT, FUNDING, DESIGN, AND EVALUATION

Since 1 January 2001 the Netherlands has had, like other European countries, a Council for the Judiciary. This Council is responsible for the development of the IT infrastructure and applications for the courts. The management of a particular court, including the decisions to use specific tools is still in the hands of each court individually. This is also the case for the funding of systems, as well as for their design and evaluation.

It is interesting to note the difference between the courts and the Public Prosecution Service. The latter is more subject to general and co-ordinated management than the Judiciary. The Ministry of Justice is responsible for the general management of the Public Prosecution Service. For the Public Prosecution Service certain systems have been developed, like COMPAS, that are generally used by all Public Prosecution offices. The spin-off of these systems are systems that are also used by judges for specific tasks. An example is the ARC system that is used by the investigating magistrate. But verdicts are also constructed with the help of data contained in COMPAS, for which a separate entry (SAS) is used by the judges. Another interesting observation is that the (management) organization of the police force resembles the (management) organization of the Judiciary. Police forces in the various districts are quite autonomous. However, the use of co-ordinated systems is limited for the police. The degree of IT support varies among the various police districts and depends on the management of a particular district. Systems are developed according to the initiative of a specific (group of) forces. The same is true for judges. The NOSTRA system, for example (see *supra* 6.2), is an initiative of the northern circuit.

Databases have traditionally been developed and exploited by publishers. The initiative, design and evaluation have always been controlled by those publishers. They have also taken the necessary financial risk. This has been a natural consequence of the fact that in the Netherlands the publication of case law and of legislation has traditionally been in the hands of commercial publishers (Bovens 1998, p. 28). This means that they could decide on the prices for their services, and what is to be published and what not. Recently this seems to have changed. When the ADW (Algemene Databank Wet- en regelgeving[6]) was published electronically, it gave rise to some commotion because of the fact that it had been exploited by a publisher and that one had to pay for its use (Verkade 1998). A special service called JUSTEX should co-ordinate the automated deliverance of case law and a special Internet site (<www.rechtspraak.nl>) has since 1999 published cases according to specific guidelines. The latter has not been developed for the courts, but for public use. Also, since 2002 a special site called Wetten.nl has been open to the public, and includes all Dutch legislation, including Ministry guidelines.

Together with the establishment of the new Council, a new nationwide service organisation for the Council for the Judiciary, the Public Prosecutions Office and – on behalf of the Supreme Court – the Ministry of Justice has been formed, the ICTRO (ICT for the Judicial Organisation).

ICTRO is in charge of maintaining the IT infrastructure for the Judiciary and the prosecution service. They install and maintain hardware, they maintain and develop software applications and they provide train-

---

[6] General database Act and regulation.

ing, but, generally speaking, policies are not directed at developing entirely new initiatives, but to make use of what others have already developed. The organisation has been set up as a service of the Ministry of Justice, but the Ministry has transferred ownership to the Council and the Prosecution Service. Assignments are given by internal contracts. This means that the Council for the Judiciary and the Public Prosecutions Department are able to supervise IT services and the development of specific IT applications.

The Judiciary has its own agency for developing new Internet and web-based applications, called BISTRO (Bureau Internet Systemen en Toepassingen Rechterlijke Organisatie). Other new IT developments will largely be realised through outsourcing. In order to steer these efforts, the Council is in the process of setting up a programme management organisation.

Recently, a project entitled 'Proeflokaal ICT' has been set up to gain an insight, on a structural basis, into the possibilities of ICT for supporting the Judiciary.

6.7   SENTENCING SYSTEMS FOR JUDGES *AND* PROSECUTORS

The movement for fairer and more consistent sentencing in the Netherlands led to the development of several JDSSs that are already or shortly will be used by the Public Prosecution Service and the Judiciary. The systems that have so far been developed are meant to be used by the Public Prosecution Service on the one hand, and the judges on the other.

The different role of the judge (independent) and the public prosecutor (belonging to the executive branch) must be reflected in the IT support. The rule-based system BOS is appropriate for the public prosecution service (formalized guidelines). The judge, however, may be more ably assisted by a different method of support: quick and easy access to information on the case at hand, instead of a database containing previous cases.

6.8   On the mandatory use of systems

The difference in organization between the Judiciary and the public prosecutors is also reflected in the mandatory use of systems. In theory, it is
easier to oblige the public prosecution service to use specific systems.
The general management task of the Ministry of Justice enhances this.
The autonomy of the courts, in the present situation, does not make such
an obligation possible. In practice we can see, however, that it is not so
easy to actually effectuate the use of systems. That also means co-operation between local management. They have to take measures to compel
the use of the system. According to our information the BOS system is
not used on a general basis by all Public Prosecution Offices.

6.9   Theoretical legal issues

IT support for administrative tasks has already existed for a long time in
the Judiciary. From a more recent date stems the use of decision support
systems (e.g., BOS) and automated decision-making (e.g., Mulder). The
validation of these types of systems is important, because these systems
decide themselves or support those who have to take such decisions. Although in the past attention has been paid to the issue of validation
(Kracht, De Vey Mestdagh and Svensson 1998, Weusten 1993), this topic
has recently gained renewed attention (e.g., De Vey Mestdagh 1999,
Oskamp 1999).

   The question of in what way the principles of traditional dispute settlement can be realized in an electronic environment is something that needs
serious consideration over the next couple of years. There are currently
initiatives by the European Union on electronic dispute settlement (both
by traditional courts and alternative dispute resolution).

   The Dutch government is still working on the implementation of the
data protection directive (95/46/EC). Privacy is an issue that influences
the exchange of data between the different parties in the judicial chain.
The exchange of data concerning a suspect between the police and the
public prosecution service is a delicate issue. More in general, the question is who should be allowed to obtain information on suspects and/or

convicted criminals and under what conditions. Precise guidelines and independent supervision are necessary on this point.

6.10   THEORETICAL ICT ISSUES

One of the theoretical ICT issues is the question to what extent, for the administration of cases, distributed local databases linked to one another through general indices should be used. The alternative would be a central database.

It is generally acknowledged that access to files and information independent from the location where a judge or prosecutor is located at a certain moment is desirable. The question here is how the remote access can be realized, and can a high level of security still be guaranteed. Since it is to be expected that criminal organizations will increasingly shift their activities to the electronic environment (cyber crime), it goes without saying that the growing expertise in ICT among criminals will have repercussions on the level of security that needs to be effectuated.

The use of advanced technologies, like data mining, intelligent agents, speech recognition and knowledge systems will become more and more integrated in the ICT of the Judiciary.

6.11   COMPLETELY DIGITIZED PROCEDURES

A so-called Document Information System (DIS) is currently being developed by the Public Prosecution Service. A DIS contains scanned and stored documents relating to criminal cases and enables authorized users to work with original documents simultaneously.[7] That authorization is to be regulated within an Intranet environment. A spin-off of the Document Information System is an automatically generated 'electronic file': an electronic version of what is normally contained in a paper file. Within the Judiciary several pilot studies have been carried out with files on a CD-ROM. It has been shown that the efficiency of recovering relevant

---

[7] Thereby re-entering the texts of official documents, e.g., in order to formulate statements as evidence is no longer necessary.

facts concerning a specific case improved, especially if a sizeable case was concerned. However, collecting information on a case on a hardly amendable CD-ROM is not the way in which it will be done in the future. Therefore other non-permanent information carriers like regular data bases are more suitable.

The DIS can produce electronic files and these files can be transported to various information systems. However, it must be regulated who has read or has access and to what part of the available information. Some parts should be accessible to the prosecutor, whereas other information should be accessible to the judge only. In the possible absence of legal prescriptions, agreements have to be made as to which of the mutations by the judge are accessible for the prosecutor and vice versa. In order to produce electronic files in an efficient way, again a uniform structure of information is essential. If the judge at first instance has decided a case that is stored in an electronic file, eventually other courts must be able to access that electronic file. In case of appeal, the court of appeal handling the case will not only have the right to access the information on the electronic file, but also the right to add relevant new information.

It should be noted that already at the beginning of the 1990s, and maybe even before then, the term paperless office was being used. However, realization of the electronic file should not to be expected in the very near future. In mid-1999 the pilot schemes of the DIS project were not really successful (Lodder, Oskamp and Duker 2000).

6.12   THE STATE OF AUTOMATION

The general state of automation of the Judiciary is reasonably satisfactory.

In criminal proceedings, the core of the administrative systems is COMPAS, which was introduced in the late 1980s. The central concept of this administrative system is a criminal case. For each new case a file is added to the system, even if there is already another case with the same suspect. Lack of knowledge concerning other cases related to the same person has in the past led to failures, for example suspects being summoned at their home address while they were actually serving a term of imprisonment. To prevent such errors a system called VIPS (Reference

Index Criminal Law) has been developed. By means of a unique number this system connects the data of a person stored in criminal proceeding systems with external systems like the registration of inhabitants by the municipalities. The VIPS system has already been operational since the mid-1990s, but its actual use is somewhat disappointing. The successor of COMPAS is currently being developed and takes a person, not a case, as its starting point. Building upon the idea of VIPS, different cases relating to the same person are stored in one file instead of separate files. Note that the COMPAS system is primarily meant for use by the public prosecution service. The judges have separate access to the system by means of the ARC and SAS systems.

In administrative procedure the BERBER administrative system was introduced at the beginning of the 1990s. Also in civil proceedings an administrative system is used, known as 'Civiel Rechtbank' (cf., Weusten et al., 1999, p. 115).

There is, however, still quite a discrepancy between the possible use of implemented systems and their actual use. For instance, the Ministry of Justice does have a Document Information System, but this system is only used to monitor the physical location of paper files. The reference in the system is either to the person who has the paper file at a particular moment, or to the archive. No electronic copies of the files can be retrieved when using the system. Another example is the BOS system, its use being obligatory for Public Offenders since April 1999. From inside information which we have obtained concerning two courts, it appeared that at the beginning of 2000 in one court the system had never be used, and in another court it was used only occasionally. We do not have the feeling that the situation in the other 17 courts will be totally different.

If we are talking about automation nowadays, we cannot discount the Internet. The Ministry of Jusitice has quite an informative site (<www. justitie.nl>), and also the Public Prosecution Service has its own site (<www.openbaarministerie.nl>). Via <www.rechtspraak.nl> information can be obtained about the courts' organisation and concerning the different procedures. On the national site guidelines for civil and administrative proceedings are published. Each court also publishes its organisational rules and various guidelines concerning different types of proceedings, and guidelines concerning costs. The courts publish a selection of their case law and a calendar of court sessions. Also the additional offices of judges are published on the courts' web site.

Via <www.openbaarministerie.nl> various information is made available to the public. The site also offers information about the administrative handling of minor offences, news, dossiers on special cases and guidelines for what degree of punishment can be demanded in most categories of cases.

6.13 BIBLIOGRAPHICAL REFERENCES

BOVENS, M.A.P. (1998), *De digitale rechtsstaat: beschouwingen over informatiemaatschappij en rechtsstaat* (inaugeral address), Utrecht

DUKER, M.J.A. AND A.R. LODDER (1999), 'Sentencing and Information Management: consistency and the particularities of a case', *Proceedings of the Seventh International Conference on Artificial Intelligence and Law*, ACM, New York, pp. 100-107

HUTTON, H. ET AL. (1996), *A Sentencing Information System for the Scottish High Court*, The Scottish Office, Central Research Unit

KOERS, A. (1999), *Driemaal is scheepsrecht* (inaugeral address), Utrecht.

KRACHT, D., C.N.J. DE VEY MESTDAGH AND J.S. SVENSSON (1998), *Legal Knowledge Based Systems: An overview of criteria for validation and practical use*, Lelystad, Koninklijke Vermande

LODDER, A.R., A. OSKAMP AND M.J.A. DUKER (2000), *Informatietechnologische ondersteuning binnen het strafprocesrecht*, ITeR No. 36, Den Haag, Sdu

OSKAMP, A. (1998), *Rechtsinformatica: vooruitzien in de informatiemaatschappij* (inaugeral address), Deventer, Kluwer

OSKAMP, A. (1999), 'Voorwaarden voor juridische IT-gebruik: beoordeling vooraf, tijdens en na ontwikkeling', in: A. Oskamp and A.R. Lodder (red.), *Informatietechnologie voor Juristen – Handboek voor de jurist in de 21ste eeuw*, Deventer, Kluwer, pp. 145-160

OSKAMP, E.W. (1998), *Computerondersteuning bij straftoemeting, de ontwikkeling van een databank*, Arnhem, Gouda Quint

POLARIS (1997), Project Ontwikkeling Landelijke Richtlijnen Strafvordering, *Brochure ter introductie van de POLARIS-richtlijnen*, Den Haag, Openbaar Ministerie Voorlichtingsdienst, Paleis van Justitie

DE VEY MESTDAGH, C.N.J. (1999), 'Validatie van juridische informatiesystemen', in: A. Oskamp and A.R. Lodder (red.), *Informatietechnologie voor Juristen – Handboek voor de jurist in de 21ste eeuw*, Deventer, Kluwer, pp. 161-177

VERKADE, D.W.F. (1998), 'Het contract is een schande', *Computerrecht* 1998/3, pp. 104-105

WEUSTEN, M.C.M. (1993), 'Validation: the key concept in maintenance of legal KBS', *Proceedings of the Fourth International Conference on Artificial Intelligence and Law*, New York, Association of Computing Machinery (ACM)

WEUSTEN, M.C.M. ET AL. (1999), *Inleiding in de juridische informatica*, Deventer, Kluwer

Chapter 7
INFORMATION AND COMMUNICATION TECHNOLOGY FOR JUSTICE: THE ITALIAN EXPERIENCE

Marco Fabri

7.1 INTRODUCTION

Until the early 1990s the design, development, and the implementation of information and communication technology (ICT) in the Italian public sector did not follow any specific plan, but were isolated answers to specific problems. In 1993, the establishment of an independent Authority for Information Technology in the Public Administration (AIPA), has favoured a more systematic approach to improve the consistency and the interoperability of the different ICT investments. In particular, in the justice sector there has been an impressive growth of ICT projects, that has not been always followed by a similar increase in running applications.

The first part of this article provides a summary description of the Italian Judiciary. Then the dramatic change in the government strategy for the development of technology in the public sector is addressed. Technology governance is actually the framework that strongly affects any technological innovation and development. In the second part, I will focus on the current main Information and Communication Technology projects and applications in the Italian justice system. It is worth mentioning that at this moment in time the number of ICT initiatives is so high that it is very difficult to have an accurate updated description of the current situation. The risk that the picture becomes outdated very soon is very great, but this is an insurmountable limit of any attempt to describe the state of Information Technology. It is also noteworthy that while data about ICT projects are relatively easy to obtain, it is rather difficult to collect infor-

A. Oskamp, et al. (Eds), IT Support of the Judiciary
© *2004, ITeR, The Hague, and the authors*

mation on the current situation concerning the real use of technology in the courts and public prosecutors' offices. This is due to the boost in the number of ICT projects, as well as the lack of an effective and accessible monitoring of the developments by the Ministry of Justice.

The third part of this paper will address a specific issue: Information and Communication Technology for court performance appraisal. In this section, I will briefly deal with the question whether ICT is used to generate management information to assess the productivity and the 'quality' of courts' work. The concluding remarks will provide some reflections on the actual situation of ICT within the Italian Judiciary.

7.2   THE ITALIAN JUDICIARY: A BRIEF OVERVIEW

The Italian Judiciary has some peculiarities that makes it quite different from the other European justice systems. In particular, in the Italian justice system public prosecutors are part of the Judiciary and not part of the executive.[1] Both judges and prosecutors are an integral part of the *magistratura*, as members of the same body they are called magistrates (*magistrati*). They have the status of a public official, and since they are considered part of traditional state bureaucracy, and during their career they can switch from prosecutorial to judge's functions as often as they like, with the consent of the Higher Council of the Magistracy. Judges and prosecutors start their career in the Judiciary when they are about twenty-seven years old (Di Federico and Guarnieri 1988). A law degree is required, and they have to enter a public competition which concentrates on their knowledge of formal and abstract law. Their careers are substantially based on seniority (Di Federico 1976).

The Higher Council of the Magistracy is the institution in charge of recruitment, promotion, transfer, and a disciplinary system for judges and prosecutors.[2] Established in 1959, after recent reform[3] it is now composed

---

[1] Prior to World War Two, prosecutors were hierarchically subordinate to the Minister of Justice. The Italian Constitution enacted after the Fascist regime placed the public prosecutors within the Judiciary setting.

[2] Italian Constitution Art. 105.

[3] Law n. 44, 28 March 2002.

of twenty-seven members: eighteen are judges and prosecutors elected by their colleagues,[4] eight are law professors or attorneys elected by Parliament, and three members are *ex officio*.[5] Every Council lasts for four years, and members cannot be immediately reappointed.[6]

The Ministry of Justice is entrusted with the organization and the functioning of the judicial offices (procurement, Information Technology, administrative personnel, budgeting, etc.).[7] It is a peculiarity of the Italian Ministry of Justice that almost all of the executive positions are held by magistrates.[8]

The Italian judicial offices are spread all over the country[9] and they are organized as follows.

The first single judge court of limited jurisdiction is presided over by the Justices of the Peace (*Giudice di Pace*). There are 849 Justices of the Peace offices nationwide, and currently they have limited jurisdiction in civil and criminal matters.[10] The court of first instance with general jurisdiction is the Tribunal (*Tribunale*). There are 166 of them all over the country, plus 222 detached offices.[11] In this court sits a single judge or a

---

[4] The elected magistrates must be: two judges who work at the Court of Cassation, ten 'ordinary' judges, and four public prosecutors. Each magistrate can vote for just one candidate from each of the three 'kinds', and the one who obtains the majority of the votes is elected.

[5] Ex officio members of the Higher Council of the Magistracy are: the President of the Republic, the President of the Court of Cassation, and the Chief of the Public Prosecutor's Office attached to the Court of Cassation.

[6] Italian Constitution Art. 104.

[7] Italian Constitution Art. 110.

[8] About 42,000 administrative personnel work in the courts, the prosecutors' offices and in the Ministry of Justice. The numbers of judges and administrative personnel who work in each court and prosecutor's office is very variable, it ranges from several hundred judges in the major courts such as Rome and Milan, to no more than ten judges in several courts (Marini 2000).

[9] Italy is not a federal State although administratively its territory is divided into twenty different regions. Italy has about 57 million inhabitants.

[10] The Justices of the Peace were introduced in the Italian justice system by law n. 374, 21 November 1991, which entered into effect in May 1995. The Justices of the Peace are lay judges appointed by the Higher Council of the Magistracy for a four-year term. Their statutory ceiling is 4,700. Initially they had only limited jurisdiction in civil matters, but since January 2002 they now also have limited jurisdiction in criminal matters.

[11] In 93 tribunals there is a special section called Corte di Assise that have jurisdiction over the most serious criminal cases. These courts have two career judges and six lay

panel of three judges, depending on the kind of case. Attached to each of the 166 courts of general jurisdiction there are 166 public prosecutors' offices.[12]

Appeals from justices of the peace go before the tribunals, while appeals from the tribunals go before the 26 courts of appeal (*Corte d'appello*) – plus three detached divisions. Attached to each court of appeal there is a public prosecutor's office. The courts of appeal have a panel of three judges, and it is important to note that the appeal process is based both on factual and legal issues.

It is worth mentioning that the current court structure only came into effect in July 1999. Up until then, there were two courts of first instance: the *pretura*, a single judge court of limited jurisdiction in civil and criminal matters and the tribunals, which were courts with general jurisdiction. After the law reform the 165 *preture* merged with the tribunals, creating a single court of first instance with general jurisdiction.

The highest court is the Court of Cassation (*Corte di Cassazione*), located in Rome, which deals with questions of law and reviews all provisional orders relating to personal liberties. The Court of Cassation is supposed to guarantee the uniform jurisprudential interpretation of the law.[13] The court must consider all the pleadings filed; it does not have a *certiorari* discretion. This feature has generated a huge case load and a gigantic court with more than 400 judges, which is very uncommon in comparison to the other highest European courts.

Criminal cases involving defendants under eighteen years of age are handled by 29 Juvenile Courts (*Tribunale dei minorenni*), which also have a specialized prosecutor's office. Members of the panel are two ca-

---

judges, acting as juriors. The appeals from these courts lie to special sections of the Court of Appeal (Corte d'Assise d'Appello).

[12] It is also important to mention that in 26 prosecutors' offices there is a special anti-mafia unit called the Direzione Distrettuale Antimafia (District Anti-mafia Bureau), established in 1992, which is charged with all mafia cases within a specific appeal district. These 26 special units are co-ordinated by a central office located in Rome, called the Direzione Nazionale Antimafia (National Anti-mafia Bureau).

[13] Although Italy is a country with a civil law tradition (so the *stare decisis* doctrine does not apply), precedents have always played a major role in sentencing. In particular, the sentences delivered by the Supreme Court of Cassation have always affected the decision-making process of the trial courts.

reer judges and two social workers, one male and one female. Appeals lie to a special section of the Court of Appeal.

Constitutional review is granted by the Constitutional Court (*Corte Costituzionale*) which has fifteen judges, each appointed for a nine-year term. Five are appointed by the President of the Republic, five by the superior Italian courts (Court of Cassation, Council of State, and Court of Account), and five are elected by Parliament. The Constitutional Court also hears conflicts which have arisen among the different branches of government.

It is important to mention that in 1989 Italy switched from an inquisitorial criminal process to a more accusatorial one (Fabri 1994, 1995). Since then several constitutional provisions as well as legislative interventions have drastically changed the original accusatorial structure, but this issue will not be further addressed here. However, it is important to note that the 1989 code erased the traditional position of the investigating judge (*giudice istruttore*) and introduced a preliminary hearing as well as several criminal special proceedings as alternatives to a full trial. It is essential to remember that another Italian peculiarity among the European criminal justice systems is the Constitutional provision of mandatory penal action,[14] meaning that any complaint received by the police must be transmitted to the prosecutor's offices. The latter cannot autonomously dismiss a case without the judge's consent.[15]

7.3   ICT GOVERNANCE IN THE ITALIAN JUDICIAL SYSTEM

The initiatives on information and communication technology in the Italian Judiciary have to be related to the framework in which the projects are developed. Not many ICT projects that are currently under way would have occurred without a new government policy on technology in the public administration that led to the creation of the AIPA.[16]

---

[14] Italian Constitution Art. 112.

[15] A specialist judge, the judge for preliminary investigation (giudice per le indagini preliminari), was introduced by the 1989 code. This judge decides on requests for dismissal or formal indictment proposed by the public prosecutor after the investigation.

[16] The Authority for Information Technology in the Public Administration (AIPA) was created by law n. 39, 1993.

The Authority was established to promote, co-ordinate, plan and control the development of information systems in all the branches of public administration. The ultimate goal was to improve the services supplied by public administrations to the citizens through the use of ICT.

In particular, the Authority strategically co-ordinated all the ICT projects in the public administration, approving the three-year ICT plan which each administration and government agency had to present to the Authority on a yearly basis. Other important tasks were the *regulatory* ones that include setting planning standards, designing and managing information systems as well as defining quality and security policies. Among the regulatory tasks the Authority also set criteria to monitor contracts related to the projects carried out by the administration. The Authority also had significant *promoting tasks* to stimulate projects that involved more administrations and to increase the development of the ICT infrastructure. Other tasks carried out by the Authority are *financial* ones. The AIPA, through both an *auditing* process and a *cost evaluation* analysis, could check the information technology procurement process followed by the administration. *Training* and, in general, the ICT knowledge transfer within the public sector were other functions developed by the AIPA. The latter was mainly pursued through technical publications and the organization of courses, workshops and seminars. The Authority was also an *advisory body* for the government. In this role, the AIPA had defined the technical rules on digital signature adopted by the Italian government.[17]

The Authority could be acknowledged as a technostructure (Mintzberg 1983), considering its standardization and planning tasks. It was actually a technostructure *sui generis*, since it could *veto* projects, but it did not really play a major role in their design, which was left to the single administrations.

However, it is worth mentioning that the new government which has ruled the country since April 2001, has created a new Ministry of Innovation and Technology to further boost the use of ICT. This Ministry, ac-

---

[17] Presidential decree n. 513, November 1997: 'Regulations establishing criteria and means for implementing section 15(2) of Law 59, March 1997, concerning the creation, storage and transmission of documents by means of computer-based or telematic systems'.

cordingly to the 'E-Government Action Plan 2002',[18] took over many of the tasks of AIPA, in order to assist the public administrations in the development of ICT projects.

The law that established the AIPA also provided for the creation of ICT Departments in each Ministry. The goal was to connect the single administrations with the Authority, also giving a new organizational structure to ICT Departments within the public administrations.

In particular, in the last years the ICT Department of the Ministry of Justice has experienced a huge growth in both budget and personnel.[19]

The executive positions of the ICT Department are held by magistrates, and the general manager of the ICT Department is also a magistrate, who has taken responsibility since its initial establishment. In addition, two magistrates are in charge of the criminal and the civil division, and a third is responsible for co-ordinating and developing, all over the country, the criminal automated case management system (Re.Ge.).[20] The fact that the executive positions of the ICT Department are occupied by magistrates should come as no surprise since it confirms the rule that sees almost all the executive positions of the Italian Ministry of Justice held by magistrates.

From the governance setting just described, it should be clear who is managing, funding, designing and evaluating the ICT projects developed in the public administrations and in the Judiciary in particular. Actually, each Ministry is in charge of designing, managing and funding its own ICT projects. The projects have to be proposed in the three-year ICT plan.

---

[18] Among the main goals of the Ministry for the public sector in 2003 are the following: the distribution of at least one billion digitial signatures within the public administration by 2003, a 50% increase in the use of e-procurement, one-third of personnel trained through e-learning, two-thirds of all public offices with on-line access for the public. 'E-Government Action Plan 2002' at <http://www.pianoegov.it>.

[19] The ICT Department of the Ministry of Justice invested about 149 million Euro in 1999, 169 milion Euro in 2000, and 202 million Euro in 2001. The Department now has more than 500 personnel such as administrative staff, information technology specialists, organizational analysts. It also has thirteen regional offices (CISIA) spread throughout the country (August 2002).

[20] Re.Ge. stands for Registri Generali, which means general docket or registry of case actions.

The strategic decision to leave the design, planning, and the implementation of the ICT projects, as well as the responsibility for ICT developments, within each branch of the administration was probably made in order to create a sort of accountability for and ownership over the projects, even if it is not really clear how this accountability can be enforced. This is particularly true for the general manager of the ICT Department of the Ministry of Justice, since the management of the magistrates is the exclusive task of the Higher Council of the Magistracy.

As far as the technology governance of the courts and prosecutors' offices is concerned, it is important also to mention the initiative taken by the Higher Council of the Magistracy. This latter body, after the institution of the ICT Department of the Ministry of Justice, has established the peculiar position of the *ICT magistrate*. In each of the 26 Italian judicial districts – with few exceptions – two *ICT magistrates*, one for the civil and one for the criminal field, have been appointed to co-ordinate, stimulate and to evaluate the ICT initiatives set out in their district. The meaning of this decision can be found in the judges' and prosecutors' perception that it is important to ensure the implementation of ICT in the judicial system, since it is still seen by some as a possible menace to their independence. Information and Communication Technology is certainly considered to be a critical issue in order to retain the actual power structure within the courts and the Ministry of Justice, therefore it cannot be relegated solely to managers or ICT specialists, but must instead receive the focused attention of the magistrates.

The creation of the Authority has dramatically changed the strategy of ICT governance in the public sector. The Authority, as a parallel learning structure (Bushe and Shani 1991), was also established to try to break down the previously fragmented ICT governance setting, that had provided very poor results and had wasted a great deal of resources in all the public administrations in the recent past. The new ICT Departments, in many cases, have actually dispensed with some traditional organizational dysfunctions, creating a more knowledgeable structure for ICT innovation in the administrations.

However, after the initial boost, the ICT Department of the Ministry of Justice has shown some tendencies to resort to the traditional bureaucratic logic of action (Friedberg 1993), thereby losing the required flexibility which is fundamental to promoting innovation processes. For example, the implementation strategy adopted by the ICT Department of the Ministry of Justice is still following a strict top-down approach, and it has not really changed even with the establishment of the regional offices. The ICT Department of the Ministry of Justice decides on ICT applications, and the use of such applications are mandatory for the courts and the prosecutors' offices all over the country.

Another major problem is that the ICT Department of the Ministry of Justice still seems to be too weak in dealing with ICT providers.[21] In particular, the Ministry of Justice seems to be too dependant on ICT providers for technical design, implementation policy, monitoring, and the development of projects as well as for technical assistance. Even though the ICT Department has recently hired system analysts and computer programmers, most of the project design as well as the information systems' maintenance and development is still outsourced. This creates major problems in interconnections among different systems as well as dysfunctional ties with vendors that tend to play a dominant role in the ICT solutions proposed to maximize their profit. The establishment of the Authority has partially mitigated this situation, but the technical weakness of the ICT Department of the Ministry of Justice is still a major problem. In addition, the salaries offered to ICT experts in the private sector are much more appealing than the ones available in the public administration. As a consequence many ICT personnel leave the administration for the private sector after a brief career in the public sector.

7.4   INFORMATION AND COMMUNICATION TECHNOLOGY IN THE JUDICIAL PROCESS

If, on the one hand, in recent years ICT projects have certainly burst into the Italian judicial system, on the other hand, the main problem is still the implementation of these numerous projects, which in many cases have become bogged down in a feasibility study or in an everlasting pilot stage.

---

[21] In this regard, it is worth mentioning that all the public administrations can now use (Presidential decree n. 101, 4 April 2002) a special government agency for e-procurement (CONSIP). See <http://www.consip.it> and <http://www.acquistinretepa.it>.

The projects concern the interest of the criminal and the civil justice systems as well as the administrative operations of both courts and prosecutors' offices, along with the Ministry of Justice. In this section I will describe some of these projects in order to provide a broad overview of what has been planned and implemented so far.

The *criminal field* has experienced a large number of changes due to two major events: the introduction of a completely new Code of criminal procedure in 1989, with an accusatorial structure that superseded the previous inquisitorial one, and the assassination of Giovanni Falcone, the General manager of the criminal affairs department of the Italian Ministry of Justice, by a mafia bomb in May 1992. The first event persuaded the Ministry of Justice to adopt a basic automated case management system that, since then, has been constantly upgraded and disseminated to all the courts and prosecutors' offices in Italy. The second, tragic event, drove the Ministry of Justice to invest resources in a fairly sophisticated database and information retrieval system specifically designed to deal with data connected with mafia crimes.

It is important to recall how these two still very important projects came into being, since the genesis of these projects highlights how the implementation of Information Technology in the Italian courts, before the institution of the AIPA, was not planned, but was the result of certain contingencies. Moreover, the following development of this software has shown a strong path dependency (Krasner 1988) that characterizes ICT initiatives.

The criminal automated case management system (Re.Ge.) is currently running in all of the 166 courts of first instance as well as in the attached prosecutors' offices, and in quite a few of the 26 courts of appeal. The software is a typical automated case management system based on a client-server architecture. The software allows limited data interchange between the courts and the prosecutor's offices. It was designed as (and still is) an automated version of the handwritten paper docket, as a register of actions within the case life from the criminal complaint up until the final sentence. Each end-user of the court or prosecutor's office has a different user ID and a password by which to access the system, and then to modify or update records. There are several different levels of passwords based on the qualification of the end-users.

In some prosecutors' offices, where the caseload is very high, the data entry can also be done by optical acquisition of the criminal complaints.

Re.Ge. was designed as a 'perfect functional equivalent' (Contini 2000) of the previous paper docket; it actually automated the *status quo* and was not projected as informing technology (Zuboff 1988). Therefore, it was not designed to assist judges and prosecutors in their decision-making process, even if in some limited cases empirical research (Fabri, Contini and Negrini 1999) has shown how courts' personnel tried to increase its potential. For example, some typical database functions were used to automate the production of standard judicial documents, and smart use of the database allowed some prosecutors to develop investigations into large-scale crimes related to car thefts.

Since its initial implementation there have already been several releases of the same software not only to meet the end-users' demands, but also to meet the numerous legal changes that have characterized Italian criminal law since the new criminal code came into effect. The implementation of these changes has been quite difficult in some cases due to the drastic modifications introduced into the procedural law by both the government and the Constitutional Court.

Judicial offices have very little margin to customize the software disseminated by the Ministry of Justice, which is in charge of its design, planning, implementation, monitoring, and development. Empirical research (Fabri, Contini and Negrini 1999) has shown how this top-down, centralized approach limits the innovation process. Actually, the initial possibility to develop some local applications autonomously by judicial personnel in courts or prosecutors' offices was particularly appreciated, generating a sense of ownership and a positive attitude towards technology. This possibility is now strongly discouraged by the ICT Department in an attempt to retain strong control over the applications all over the country, and also to prevent security problems.

Connected to Re.Ge. the ICT Department is developing some office automation applications in order to simplify the production of documents by judges and prosecutors but, as far as I know, they are not really used by more than a few courts that have tested them. This is further evidence of the limits in adopting a centralized approach in the management of ICT initiatives.

The second system which is worth mentioning is the database used by anti-mafia prosecutors. As mentioned previously, Italy has a special unit of prosecutors which have a central bureau in Rome (*Direzione Nazionale Antimafia*) and 26 prosecutors' district offices (*Direzione Distrettuale Antimafia*), which correspond to the 26 districts of the court of appeal. These anti-mafia units use a specifically designed standard query language (SQL) database (SIDNA and SIDDA)[22] which assists the prosecutors in their investigations by means of a quite powerful information retrieval system. This system underwent a significant development after the killing of Giovanni Falcone, and it was used in Sicily to collect and then retrieve evidence and information in that specific investigation. Since then, the application has been implemented in all of the 26 district offices and in the central Rome bureau where all the information concerning mafia crime is processed. The communication between the local units and the central bureau is still one of the major problems of the working system. Very often important information is not transmitted to Rome from the regional offices in order to preserve the absolute secrecy of the information. In addition, the data entry process, and its indexing, is still extremely cumbersome and this prejudices the effectiveness of the investigation.

These are the two applications that are currently running in the Italian criminal judicial offices. Many other projects are under way, and they will be briefly described, but it is important to point out that there is a huge gap between what has been projected and what has actually been implemented so far. This is certainly the most important problem which the Ministry of Justice has to address. Actually, the number of ICT projects for courts and prosecutors' offices that are currently under way is indeed impressive. The following is a non-exhaustive list thereof.

In several prosecutors' offices there has been a pilot project concerning automated case management for the execution of sentences. This is one of the most troublesome areas in the criminal field, since the flourishing of different laws creates many difficulties in computing the most

---

[22] SIDNA stands for 'Sistema Informativo Direzione Nazionale Antimafia', 'Information System for Anti-mafia National Bureau'. SIDDA stands for 'Sistema Informativo Direzione Distrettuale Antimafia', 'Information System for Anti-mafia District Bureau'.

appropriate length of the sentences as well as keeping the software constantly updated (RES-Re.Ge.).[23]

Related to this project is the information system (SITUS)[24] specifically designed for surveillance judges (*magistrati di sorveglianza*), who are in charge of supervising prisons and their inmates. This system has been piloted in a few offices and now it is supposed, after several changes, to be implemented in a few others.

An upgrade of the really outdated National Criminal History Record System (*Casellario Giudiziario*) has also been planned. The system is supposed to be an updated national database containing both convictions and formal indictments relating to defendants.[25]

Other ICT projects and applications are also under way for the benefit of the Department of Prisons, for the specific needs of the Juvenile Courts and for the Justices of the Peace, for the internal organization of the Court of Cassation as well as for the Ministry of Justice.

Among the communication technology used in the judicial process, the video conferencing systems are worth mentioning. These systems were initially installed to videotape court hearings when Italy adopted an accusatorial code of criminal procedure, when the court record became an important part of the court proceedings. The systems, as trial records, have not been very successful, but they have been progressively used as video conferencing systems in mafia trials to connect courtrooms and prisons as well as courtrooms and remote sites where witnesses are kept for security reasons.[26]

In the field of *civil law*, probably less applications have been implemented to date, in comparison with criminal law, but many projects are nevertheless under way. There are still a few outdated civil case management systems based on a mainframe architecture, which were tested in a few cities in the late 1970s. These systems should shortly be replaced by automated case management systems based on a client-server architecture

---

[23] RES stands for 'Registri esecuzioni', 'Execution registry of action'.

[24] SITUS stands for 'Sistema Informativo Tribunali e Uffici di Sorveglianza', 'Information Systems for Tribunals and Surveillance Offices'.

[25] The need to keep track of formally indicted defendants was introduced by the 1989 code of criminal procedure. It is still a major problem to make this information available to all the courts and prosecutors' offices in the country.

[26] Video conferencing in mafia trials was introduced by law n. 11, 7 January 1998.

and an Oracle database. Pilot schemes have been already used in a couple of courts and the software has been progressively disseminated to the other Italian courts.

Similar automated case management systems have recently been introduced at the offices of the Justices of the Peace.

In the civil law field, it is certainly worth mentioning a project (POLIS) that has been piloted in some courts and that has been finalized to create a database containing sentences of both the court of first instance and the court of the appeal of a particular district. Some sentences, as well as limited access to the stage of the proceedings, are already available on the web for remote access by lawyers (POLIS WEB). One of the most relevant difficulties at this moment in time is not technology, but the need to persuade judges to work with a personal computer in order to insert the sentences in the data base, as well as to change the organizational workflow. This application should be progressively extended to the other courts and be connected to the case management systems but, once again, the step between the pilot stage and the actual software dissemination seems to be always a very difficult one in the Italian experience.

POLIS, and POLIS WEB, should also be further developed to implement a 'full civil proceeding on-line'.[27] This is the most ambitious project in the civil law field, which is also connected to a large diffusion of digital signatures.

One of the projects that cuts across both the civil and the criminal fields is the development of the database of the Court of Cassation, which contains European Union, State, and regional legislation, as well as the case law of the Court of Cassation, the Constitutional Court, the Council of State, and the Court of Account. Traditionally, the Court of Cassation has been the only court to provide electronic access to abstracts of its sentences through information retrieval software (Italgiure-Find) based on mainframe technology. This service is available for free to judges and prosecutors and upon payment to all other users. The system should shortly migrate to a client-server architecture, with a more user-friendly interface as well as a more powerful full-text research engine. In addition,

---

[27] Presidential decree n. 123 of 13 February 2001 has established the so-called 'technical rules' to implement the 'civil proceedings on-line'.

an XML (eXtensible Markup Language) scheme has also been used to tag the sentences of the Court of Cassation.

CD-ROMs with the complete texts of Court of Cassation sentences from recent years have been recently supplied to judges and prosecutors, while CD-ROMs containing the Italian law are provided by private publishers and are disseminated among legal professionals.

On this issue the Ministry of Justice is also carrying out, together with other public administrations, a project (*'norme in rete'*, 'laws in the net') to create an Internet Portal to search law documents through the world wide web. The portal is already accessible at <www.normeinrete.it>, but several improvements are still needed. In the future the documents should use the XML standard to tag data and then to enable the search engine to locate information more accurately.

Besides the *'norme in rete'* project the Ministry of Justice is carrying out several projects with other public administrations to share information which is of common interest. But, as far as I know, very few local applications have really worked so far (e.g., a connection to the city council registry office).

The nationwide 'Public Administration's Unified Network' (RUPA)[28] should foster the development of electronic data interchange, but so far this has not been the case. Actually in Italy, by law,[29] it would already be possible to exchange documents electronically but the necessary working procedures to make this happen have not yet been adopted. The law allows the electronic transmission of documents among public administrations and private organizations or citizens. Technical rules[30] were enacted to set up the rules for the use of the digital signature[31] and at this point in

---

[28] The RUPA project ('Rete Unica per la pubblica amministrazione') was approved by the Council of Ministers on 5 September 1995 (*Official Gazette* n. 272 November 1995). It supplies a broad band for the public administration's network. RUPA stands for 'Public Administration's Unified Network'.

[29] Presidential decree n. 513, 10 November 1997.

[30] Council of Ministers decree, 8 February 1997: 'Technical rules to implement Presidential decree n. 513, 10 November 1997'.

[31] 'Digital signature means the result of a computer-based process (validation) implementing an asymmetric cryptographic system consisting of a public and a private key, whereby the signer asserts, by means of the private key, and the recipient verifies, by means of the public key, the origin and integrity of a single electronic document or a set of such a documents'. Presidential decree n. 513, 10 November 1997, 1/b.

time seven companies have been authorized to act as the certification authorities[32] of public keys. The Ministry of Justice, as is the case with all the public agencies, according to the technical rules, 'shall on [its] own authority, generate, store, certify and use [its] own public keys'.[33]

Technically, it would be possible to file a case to a court, at least in those courts that have a good ICT infrastructure. However, to date the absence of procedures as well as the slow pace in the implementation of digital signatures have not yet allowed judicial electronic data interchange.[34] As mentioned above, in a pilot scheme court attorneys can only check the status of their proceedings by remote access. The security of the systems, data, and documents is still considered to be of such paramount importance to the courts, that the initial enthusiasm concerning judicial electronic data interchange has waned. The more important issues that have to be addressed in each country are known, and the systems must guarantee the authenticity of the sender, the integrity of the document and non-repudiation, meaning that the sender cannot repeatedly claim that the document has not been sent or that its content was different (Walker 1999).

In an attempt to maximize the security features of the systems, the Ministry of Justice has also commenced a project to supply personal computer users with a smart card, in which the user's private key is housed. The smart card should address the problem of identifying the authenticity of the person who has access to the network system.

A 'Justice Unified Network' (RUG)[35] is already operational as a subnetwork of the National public administration's unified network. At this point in time, judges and prosecutors, through the Justice Unified Network, have access to the National Criminal History Record, the database of the Court of Cassation, and the database of the Department of Prisons,

---

[32] 'Certification authority means the public or private entity that affects the certification, issues the public key certificate, makes the public key and the corresponding certificate publicly available, and publishes and updates certificate suspension and revocation lists'. Presidential decree n. 513, 10 November 1997, 1/k.

[33] Presidential decree n. 513, 10 November 1997, 17/1.

[34] It is worth mentioning that the plans of the Ministry of Justice entail giving a digital signature to all judicial personnel (about 42,000 people) by 2005. A few thousand have already been distributed during 2002.

[35] RUG stands for 'Rete Unica Giustizia', 'Justice Unified Network'.

as well as to e-mail services.[36] The Ministry of Justice is willing to increase the services available on this network as soon as possible (e.g., electronic mail, FTP services, etc.).

The Italian Ministry of Justice also has a web site (<www.giustizia. it>), which contains a substantial amount of information, but it does not really exploit all the available potential.

7.5   INFORMATION AND COMMUNICATION TECHNOLOGY FOR COURT PERFORMANCE APPRAISAL

Information and communication technology should improve the availability of reliable data in order to generate reports which are useful in running the courts and the prosecutors' offices, and to support managerial decisions such as the correct evaluation of needs and their best allocation within the offices. Generally, the reports answer some basic questions such as: how many cases are processed by a court during a specified period; what kind of cases are being processed by the court; how long does it take to process the cases, at what stage of processing can each case be found; how many resources (time, effort, personnel, and money) are needed to process cases and who processes them. Typical management reports are: a caseload inventory, the manner of disposition, trend analysis, the age of cases, the status of cases, exception reports, time standards, the time between specific events, and specific reports for the types of cases and judges.

It is quite common in all organizations to experience personnel inertia in monitoring activities, as well as some difficulties in changing sceptical attitudes towards data analysis. However, in the Italian Judiciary several obstacles have so far characterized the implementation of management information systems or workflow tools. The most important difficulties quite often emanate from judges and prosecutors, who view the implementation of data monitoring systems as a possible threat to judicial independence. Even highlighting the performance of judges and prosecutors is a very sensitive issue in the Italian judicial 'ivory tower'. The circula-

---

[36] In 2002, the Ministry of Justice already had over 24,000 e-mail accounts (August 2002).

tion of data is generally perceived by magistrates as a threat to their independence because it could introduce a form of control over their activities, and as a consequence it is extremely difficult to obtain information
about the performance of courts and prosecutors' offices.

At this point in time, the criminal automated case management system
which has been implemented in the majority of courts and prosecutors'
offices has a built-in statistical package, but it is not really used to monitor either the quantity or the quality of decisions delivered by judges or
prosecutors.

On a regular basis, civil case statistics are also collected by the Ministry of Justice that publishes, in collaboration with the National Institute of
Statistics, a collection of data for each district, but these data are not used
for management purposes, neither by the Ministry of Justice nor by the
Higher Council of the Magistracy.

It is noteworthy that judicial statistics are a perfect example of how the
implementation of the same case management system in the various
courts and prosecutors' offices has not been sufficient to standardize internal procedures and data collection. For this, and also for other reasons
that can not be addressed here, the quality of court statistics is generally
considered quite poor, providing an additional argument to the judges and
court personnel who do not want some kind of performance appraisal. Although the resistance to a good data reporting system is still considerable,
some policy makers from the Ministry of Justice are aware of the importance in having a reliable management information system, and therefore
the Ministry has instigated a feasibility study to implement a justice data
warehouse with a good capability for data mining.

With reference to this issue, it is worth mentioning a common project
between the Ministry of Justice and the Higher Council of the Magistracy
on the definition of criteria to evaluate the performance of courts, judges,
and prosecutors. Since 1999, a study group composed of magistrates and
consultants, appointed by both the Minister of Justice and the Higher
Council of the Magistracy,[37] has been working on the establishment of a

---

[37] The Higher Council of the Magistracy has its own Intranet and a data-base to manage the allocation, transfer, and promotion of judges and prosecutors. The Council has
also recently implemented a workflow tool to manage the cumbersome paperwork that
characterizes its institutional activities.

set of variables to monitor the functioning and the performance of judicial offices. In July 2002, the study group released its first report. The report underlines that at this stage statistics are not sufficient to have a reliable monitoring system, so a great deal of emphasis and hope rely on improving the quality of data, thanks to the progressive implementation of better automated case management systems. The report also stresses the complexity in evaluating judicial performance due to the different actors within the judicial process (i.e., judges, administrative personnel, lawyers, police forces, etc.), as well as the large variety of judicial proceedings and case types. Nevertheless, several activities by judges and prosecutors are not always related to a specific case, creating further difficulties in performance assessment. However, a first list of four variables, and several related indicators, were identified to monitor the performance of first instance civil and criminal courts, and their attached prosecutors' offices. These variables and related indicators should shortly be tested in few courts and prosecutors' offices.

Another issue that is going to persuade the Ministry of Justice to implement a better management information system is the management accounting policy, that has been introduced in the public sector by the government.[38] This is also supposed to persuade the Ministry of Justice to take responsibility for cost control, financial analysis and, in general, administrative workflow. Needless to say, there are already feasibility studies on several issues that deal with management accounting, but no application is currently in place in the courts or in the Ministry of Justice.

7.6   CONCLUDING REMARKS

The establishment of the AIPA certainly contributed in boosting the development of ICT projects in the public administrations in general, in the Ministry of Justice, and in the courts. The evaluation of infrastructure, hardware investment, and the new rules enacted can certainly be positive, but a great deal still has to be done as regards software applications, training and project management. Unfortunately, the gap between what has been projected and what has actually been realized to date is still very

---

[38] Law n. 59, 1997.

wide. Actually, the working applications that are currently in place in the Italian courts and prosecutors' offices are very few, considering the huge numbers of projects and in comparison with some other European countries (Fabri and Contini 2001). In the Italian courts there are many feasibility studies, initiatives, pilot schemes and prototypes, but the number of working systems is still quite low in a large number of judicial offices. We could say that within the Italian Judiciary 'everything is feasible, but few things are realizable'. This lack of visible results is already generating a dangerous mistrust concerning the ICT capability to improve the quality of work and then the quality of justice.

At least in the Italian courts, ICT has not yet been the instigator of change that many policy makers expected it to be. Several factors can be mentioned in this respect. For example, to have magistrates in almost all the executive positions of the Ministry of Justice, as well as their managerial role in the courts and prosecutors' offices, has not helped the innovation process. With very few exceptions, they have shown a deep-rooted incompetence (Veblen 1954; Argyris and Schön 1992) in dealing with organizational matters, innovation processes and change. Magistrates have not been trained to be project managers, to cope with the complexity of innovation processes, and their legal background on the contrary, quite often operates as a barrier to organizational change.

Moreover, most of the time this professional group – with a few significant exceptions – has activated organizational defences (Argyris 1990) that have further limited ICT development. It is a matter of fact that ICT initiatives are faced with the same problem of the many judicial reforms that have taken place in the last decade in Italy: strong domination by a highly independent and powerful professional group (Schön 1983). Technology has not really challenged the actual organizational structures (Barely 1986; Orlikowski and Robey 1991), the structure of power (Weick 1990; Garvin 1993), the procedures, the micro-ecology of actions (Bateson 1972), and ICT has not so far produced any perceived improvements in the justice system's performance[39] as well as any significant organizational change. The judicial organization does not seem to

---

[39] Italy has probably the largest backlog and the slowest pace of litigation, both criminal and civil, among all the Western countries. Because of the excessive duration of trials Italy has been repeatedly condemned by the European Court of Human Rights.

be able to enhance a learning process (Senge 1990), while it has become entrenched in old procedures, practices, routines, and power structure.

The risk of a goal displacement in the introduction of information technology is very high. The introduction of information technology is not a goal in itself, but it should bring a perceived benefit to the functioning of the courts such as: more visibility, more accountability, better quality within decisions, more expeditious litigation, and a decrease in costs.

Another issue is the lack of project evaluation. The Judiciary has been quite poor at evaluating and measuring the actual contribution made by technology to the administration of justice. This is even more so for the impact on the 'quality of justice'. These are the areas in which the greatest improvements are needed, as the Italian Judiciary struggles with the bewildering range of choices that technology provides. Technology is a great opportunity to support the judicial process and a stimulus for the revision of old and dysfunctional practices, but it is not a 'plug and play' tool. It needs to be carefully sustained and placed in the correct institutional governance setting in order to give rise to a positive organizational outcome. The greatest obstacle to progress is only in part the maturity of the technology, to a greater degree it is the capacity of the pertinent institutions and organizations to make the changes to the actual working practices and attitudes which are needed to reap the benefits that technology can offer.

7.7 BIBLIOGRAPHICAL REFERENCES

ARGYRIS, C. (1990), *Overcoming Organizational Defense*, Allyn & Bacon

ARGYRIS, C. AND D. SCHÖN (1978), *Organizational Learning: A Theory of Action Perspective.* Reading, MA., Addison-Wesley

ARGYRIS, C. AND D. SCHÖN (1992), *Organizational Learning*, Reading, MA., Addison Wesley

AUGUSTO, A. (2002), *National Report of Italy*, paper presented at the seminar 'Judicial Electronic Data Interchange in European Civil Proceedings and Criminal Matters: Applications, Policies and Trends', Research Institute on Judicial Systems, Bologna, Italy, 11-12 October 2002

BARELY, STEPHEN (1986), 'Technology as an Occasion for Structuring: Evidence from Observations of CT Scanners and the Social Order of Radiology Department', in *Administrative Science Quarterly*, n. 31, 78-108

BUSHE, G. AND A.B. SHANI (1991), *Parallel Learning Structures*, Reading, MA., Addison-Wesley

CONTINI, F. (2000), 'Reinventing the Docket, Discovering the Database', in M. Fabri and P. Langbroek (Eds.), *The Challenge of Change of Judicial Systems. Developing a Public Administration Perspective*, Amsterdam, IOS Press

DI FEDERICO, G. (1976), 'The Italian Judicial Profession and its Bureaucratic Setting', *The Judicial Review. The Law Journal of Scottish Universities*, 40-57

DI FEDERICO, G. AND C. GUARNIERI (1988), 'The Courts in Italy', in Waltman and Hollans (Eds.), *The Political Role of Law Courts in Modern Democracies*, London, Macmillan, 171

FABRI, M. (1994), *Theory versus practice of Italian criminal justice reform*, in 'Judicature', Vol. 77, n. 4, 211-216

FABRI, M. (1995), 'The Criminal Process in Italy after the 1989 Reform', Commentary from Conference of Supreme Courts of the Americas, Washington D.C., October 1995, in *Saint Louis University Law Journal*, Vol. 40, n. 4, 1045-1048; 1215-1218

FABRI, M., F. CONTINI AND A. NEGRINI (1999), *Progettazione organizzativa e information technology nell'amministrazione giudiziaria italiana*, 'Working paper IRSIG-CNR', Bologna, Lo Scarabeo, n. 9

FABRI, M. AND F. CONTINI (2001) (Eds.), *Justice and Technology in Europe: How ICT is Changing the Judicial Business*, The Hague, the Netherlands

FRIEDBERG, E. (1993), *Le pouvoir et la règle. Dynamiques de l'action organisée*, Paris, Edition du Seuil

GARVIN, D. (1993), 'Building a Learning Organization', *Harvard Business Review*, July-August, 78-91

KRASNER, S.D. (1988), 'Sovereignty: An Institutional Perspective', *Comparative Political Studies*, 21, 66-94

MARINI, L. (2000), 'The System of Justice in Italy: Signs of Evolution', in M. Fabri and P. Langbroek (Eds.), *The Challenge of Change of Judicial Systems. Developing a Public Administration Perspective*, Amsterdam, IOS Press

MINTZBERG, H. (1979), *The Structure of Organizations*, Englewood Cliffs, NJ., Prentice Hall

ORLIKOWSKI, W.J. AND D. ROBEY (1991), 'Information Technology and the Structuring of Organizations', in *The Institute of Management Sciences*, June, 143-169

SCHÖN, D. (1983), *The Reflective Practitioner. How Professionals Think in Action*, New York, NY, Basic Books

SENGE, P. (1990), *The Fifth Discipline. The Art and Practice of the Learning Organization*, New York, NY, Doubleday Currency

WALKER, D. (1999), *Electronic Court Documents. An Assessment of Judicial Electronic Document and Data Interchange Technology*, Williamsburg, VA., National Center for State Courts

WEICK, KARL (1990), 'Technology as Equivoque: Sensemaking in New Technologies', in Goodman P., Sproull L. and Associates (Eds.), *Technology and Organizations*, San Francisco, Jossey Bass, 1-43

Appendix 1
THE QUESTIONNAIRE 2001

The following questionnaire was sent to the authors outside Europe.

Questionnaire IT Support of the Judiciary

1. Regarding the Judiciary, how is the Judiciary organised in your country?

   For instance, the number of courts, the different types of courts (e.g., courts of appeal) and the position of the public prosecution.

2. Regarding Information Technology (IT), what are the most pressing issues brought to the legal, political and academic fora?

   Possible pressing issues:
   - *The (mandatory) use of (identical) IT-systems by judges and public prosecutors.*

   For instance, because of the different (independent) role, judges and prosecutors are not always allowed to use the same information on, e.g., the defendant.
   - *The level of courtroom automation.*
   - *The drawbacks of introducing IT.*
   - *The initiation of IT projects.*

   For instance, judges or prosecutors may come with a request for IT support, or an organisation develops systems (e.g., software houses or IT & Law research institutes) and offers them to the courts.
   - *The way IT systems for the courts are developed.*

   For instance, the use of special system development methodologies, and the involvement of certain parties (e.g., judges, software houses or IT & Law research institutes) with different influences.
   - *The influence of IT on criminal legislation and legal practice.*

   For instance, laws are or will be changed due to computer systems used during prosecution/trial, or judges and public prosecutors work differently because they are being supported by IT. Another influence could be that IT affects the discretionary power/margin of appreciation of judges/public prosecutors.

- *Trends in IT.*

For instance, intelligent and autonomous operating systems (agents), or the use of new Internet languages like XML on the short or long term within the area of criminal law.

3. Regarding (legal) information/knowledge management, what are the most pressing issues brought to the legal, political and academic fora?
    Possible pressing issues:
    - *Use of legal information/knowledge systems.*
    - *Use of information/knowledge management systems.*
    - *Use of information/knowledge departments.*
    - *Use of statistical information.*
    Please give us your opinion on the beneficiary effects that these discussions will have.

4. Additional remarks

Appendix 2
THE QUESTIONNAIRE 2000

The following questionnaire was sent to the authors outside Europe. The reports (Norway, the Netherlands, Italy) are updated until March 2003.

Questionnaire IT Support of the Judiciary

Could you indicate which of the following initiatives are or have been carried out in your country concerning IT support (e.g., decision support systems, databases):

1. to be used by judges for sentencing decisions?

2. to be used by the prosecutor for sentencing requests?

3. to be used by judges for determining damages, in particular concerning injuries?

4. Is IT used to generate management information in order to evaluate the productivity and/or quality of judges?

5. managing the initiatives;
   funding of the initiatives;
   design of the systems;
   evaluation of the initiatives.

6. Could in your country the systems (1) and (2) be identical?

7. Can the use of the systems (1-4) be made mandatory (and who would be the authority to make it so?).

8. Could you give a short impression of the systems for office automation in the court rooms of your country?

9. Is there any difference in IT tools for support between criminal and civil processes?

10. Are legal databases used in the courtrooms? If so, could you describe them?

11. How would you describe/evaluate the present state of automation of the courts in your country?

ABOUT THE AUTHORS

APISTOLA, M.
e-mail: m.apistola@rechten.vu.nl
Martin Apistola is a researcher at the Computer/Law Institute of the Vrije Universiteit Amsterdam. His Ph.D. research concerns the use and development of methods, techniques and IT for legal knowledge management.
In December 2003 he was granted the JURIX award for the best Master thesis 2001-2002 in the domain of legal informatics. JURIX (<www.jurix. nl>) is the Foundation for Legal Knowledge Based Systems.

FABRI, M.
e-mail: mfabri@irsig.cnr.it
Marco Fabri is a senior researcher at the Research Institute on Judicial Systems,[1] National Research Council, Bologna, Italy.

HAGEDAL, M.S.
e-mail: morten@hagedal.no
Morten S. Hagedal is currently working as a project manager for LOVISA, the new Case Management System for the Norwegian District Courts and the Courts of Appeal. He holds a Norwegian Law Degree (cand.jur) and an LL.M. in Computer and Information Technology Law from the University of Strathclyde. Previously he has been, *inter alia*, a lecturer, a judge, and a

---

[1] The National Research Council's Institute on Judicial Systems aims to study and conduct research in the field of judicial administration in Italy and abroad, both as a scientific endeavour and as a service for the promotion of a better administration of justice. In contrast with the dominant formalistic approach to the study of legal institutions, the research activities conducted by the Research Institute on Judicial Systems are not confined to merely studying the body of norms that formally define and regulate the structure and functioning of judicial systems. They are directed primarily towards analysing and evaluating the actual working methods and performance of the various components of those systems, such as: courts, prosecutor's offices, Ministries of Justice, judicial councils, and organizations for the training and continuing education of judicial personnel and lawyers. A special research interest concerns ICT in the justice systems.

Deputy Director General with the Department of Courts Administration at the Ministry of Justice.

HOOGEN, R.H. VAN DEN
e-mail: ronald@rechtspleging.nl
Ronald van den Hoogen is a former teacher and researcher at the University of Utrecht. His interest lies both in IT Law (Internet law, e-commerce, AI & Law) and in the organisation of the Judiciary. He is working on a Ph.D. project on the introduction of IT in the Judiciary. From November 2002, he is working for the Ministry of Justice of the Netherlands (Directie Strategie Rechtspleging).

JIMÉNEZ, R.
e-mail: rjimenez@tsj.gov.ve
Ricardo Jiménez Dan is an Attorney and Systems Engineer. He is Acting Executive Director for Venezuela's Supreme Tribunal's Executive Directorship. He has acted as Information Technology Director at Venezuela's Supreme Tribunal. He also managed Venezuela's Justice Modernization Programme in execution of the Agreement sustained between that country and the World Bank. Has been a Professor of Law and New Technologies at Venezuela's School for the Judiciary. He also designed and developed, the flagship web site for Venezuela's Judiciary and the Supreme Tribunal.

LODDER, A.R.
e-mail: lodder@rechten.vu.nl
Arno R. Lodder heads the IT Law section of the Computer/Law Institute of the Vrije Universiteit Amsterdam, and is also affiliated to the AI & Law section. He is the editor of several books, recently amongst others *IT Support of the Judiciary in Europe* (2001), *eDirectives: Guide to European Union Law on E-Commerce* (2002), *IT voor juristen* (second edition, 2002), and *Jurisprudentie Internetrecht* (2003). His research interests lie both in AI & Law (in particular legal argumentation, and IT Law (E-commerce), and at the intersection of both fields: Online Dispute Resolution. He is the book review editor of *AI & Law*, treasurer of JURIX, member of the UN expert committee on ODR, and director of the Centre of Electornic Dispute Resolution (CEDIRE).

OSKAMP, A.
e-mail: a.oskamp@jur.kun.nl; a.oskamp@rechten.vu.nl
Anja Oskamp is Professor of legal informatics both at the Computer/Law Institute of the Vrije Universiteit Amsterdam and the University of Nijmegen. She is the Editor-in-Chief of the Dutch Computer/Law Journal (*Computerrecht*) and *AI & Law*. In 2001 she co-edited the ITeR report *IT Support of the Judiciary in Europe*. In 2002 she edited, together with Arno Lodder, the second edition of the Dutch handbook on legal informatics.

THIAN YEE SZE
e-mail: THIAN_Yee_Sze@supcourt.gov.sg
Thian Yee Sze is Assistant Registrar of the Supreme Court in Singapore.

WALLACE, A.
email: a.wallace@unimelb.edu.au
Anne Wallace is Deputy Executive Director of the Australian Institute of Judicial Administration (AIJA) where her research interests include courtroom technology and legal systems. Together with Jeff Leeuwenburg, she has authored two reports on the use of technology in Australian courts (*Technology for Justice* and *Technology for Justice 2000*). She also organised two national conferences on this topic. She has written several papers on associated issues including 'Electronic Court Records – Privacy and Access' and 'Technology in Criminal Courts'.

List of workshop participants

In addition to the above authors, the following also participated in the workshop on 15 June 2001 in Leiden, the Netherlands.

MARC VAN OPIJNEN	The Netherlands	m.van.opijnen@fdro.drp.minjus.nl
DORY REILING	The Netherlands	d.reiling@fdro.drp.minjus.nl
AERNOUT SCHMIDT	The Netherlands	a.h.j.schmidt@law.leidenuniv.nl

INDEX

INFORMATION TECHNOLOGY & LAW SERIES

1. E-Government and its Implications for Administrative Law – Regulatory Initiatives in France, Germany, Norway and the United States (The Hague: T·M·C·ASSER PRESS, 2002)
   Editor: J.E.J. Prins / ISBN 90-6704-141-6
2. Digital Anonymity and the Law – Tensions and Dimensions (The Hague: T·M·C·ASSER PRESS, 2003)
   Editors: C. Nicoll, J.E.J. Prins and M.J.M. van Dellen / ISBN 90-6704-156-4
3. Protecting the Virtual Commons – Self-Organizing Open Source and Free Software Communities and Innovative Intellectual Property Regimes (The Hague: T·M·C·ASSER PRESS, 2003)
   Authors: R. van Wendel de Joode, J.A. de Bruijn and M.J.G. van Eeten / ISBN 90-6704-159-9
4. IT Support and the Judiciary – Australia, Singapore, Venezuela, Norway, The Netherlands and Italy (The Hague: T·M·C·ASSER PRESS, 2004)
   Editors: A. Oskamp, A.R. Lodder and M. Apistola / ISBN 90-6704-168-8

Forthcoming

- Electronic Signatures – Authentication Technology from a Legal Perspective